The Credit Movement:

For a Better Financial Future

D1528999

Ryan David

Ryan David

DISCLAIMER

"The Credit Movement" contains personal and professional references by Ryan David and others in The Credit Movement Community. Instructions are provided throughout the book and you should use your discretion in applying them to your own unique situation. You are solely responsible for any action (or inaction) taken as a result of the instruction provided. We are not lawyers, and as such, any examples, lessons, or suggestions should not be constituted as "legal advice". By continuing on with this program, you are agreeing that the tools provided are to educate yourself regarding your options and take the necessary actions for your situation. Please disregard this material if you do not agree to the above statement.

The Credit Movement Inc. expressly disclaims all warranties as to the contents of this electronic book, online courses and social networking community including, without limitation, the implied warranties of merchantability, fitness for a particular purpose, infringement, and makes no warranty as to the results that may be achieved by using the information contained in this publication or within our online properties. Because this information can be used in a variety of ways to fit various purposes, The Credit Movement Inc. will

Ryan David

Table of Contents

Chapter 3: Disputing Items for Removal   48

Chapter 5: Building Positive, Open, Active Credit 122

INTRODUCTION

About this Book, Courses, and The Community

This book should serve as a guide along your journey to better credit. You also have free access for 30 days from the purchase date of this book to utilize our membership site which includes: access to our many online courses, Video Archive, and Document Vault. Throughout the book, we will be referring to the online courses. Credit scoring and the credit improvement process is a very complex thing. There are many variables involved in dealing with the items hindering your credit. This book will give you all the tools you need to be successful. The courses that are available through our membership site will give you even more in depth guidance on how to address your unique situation and credit related goal. The private Facebook page - https://facebook.com/groups/movementacademy, is full of up-to-date credit information, live coaching sessions, and other reader interaction. Many readers of this book and users of the online courses are sharing their experiences throughout the process that could benefit others in the community —- we encourage you to introduce yourself with hashtag #ReadyToRoll.

Key Notes

This book will provide you a step-by-step guide to improving your credit by dealing with your debt and collections, student loan issues, evictions, building and maintaining positive credit and much, much more. It is imperative that you follow each step as it could determine whether you will succeed or fail. That being said, I understand that many of you will cheat and choose your own adventure. That is ok. The table of contents does allow you the ability to skip to chapters that best suit your needs. Remember, I have helped thousands of consumers and have dealt with every situation imaginable over the past decade plus. This book and the courses shares everything I have learned in a clear, concise, and actionable way.

Please always report your successes to The Facebook Community. If you haven't done so already, request access to The Credit Movement Community by visiting https://facebook.com/groups/movementacademy If you are not utilizing Facebook, email your successes to **Support@onlinetraining1.com.** Many of our readers that do not use Facebook have elected to set up an account so they may access the community and learn from what other folks are going through.

The Credit Movement History

I started The Credit Movement, wrote this book, built you various online courses, and started the online interactive community to share with you the knowledge and experience I have gained over the past 12 years. The Credit Movement puts all that experience into an easy-to-follow, step-by-step guide to a better understanding of credit with methods to remove items that don't belong on your report and improve your credit score once and for all.

I have been obsessed with our credit scoring system for the past 12 years and my personal mission is to end credit and financial suffering for ALL.

The Purpose of the Credit Scoring System

The credit scoring system in our country was designed to measure risk — your ability to pay back a loan. Credit scores are used to determine eligibility for loans or other considerations such as; utilities, cell phone service, employment, etc. Your credit score also determines the amount you will pay in interest or insurance premiums.

Unfortunately, in many ways, the credit scoring system has failed us. Various independent and government studies have revealed that credit reports are fraught with errors and oversights.

These mistakes include incorrect personal information such as names and aliases, mailing addresses, account numbers, balances, account codes, open dates, reporting dates, dates of last activity, dates of first delinquency, or dates of last activity.

The credit bureaus must obey the laws, including the Fair Credit Reporting Act (FCRA). We will share with you many loopholes and techniques to delete information on your credit report that is incomplete, inaccurate, or unverifiable.

Why So Many Different Scores?

Did you Know? There are countless algorithms or score calculations used to generate a consumer credit score. I always say, "If you go to 100 different places to view your credit score, you are likely to get 100 different scores — even with the exact same information on your report".

Credit Karma is a commonly used consumer credit report and score application. Credit Karma uses the VantageScore. Many of our readers have reported that their Credit Karma score was 50 or more points higher than what the mortgage lender pulled up for them — even with the exact same data reflecting. The reason, mortgage scores are approved by the folks who set underwriting and lending guidelines, such as Fannie Mae and Freddie Mac. The approved mortgage scores are FICO Classic (04), Fair Isaac V2, and Fair Isaac V5 FACTA.

Keep Good Records

The Credit Movement provides several Online Courses through our Membership Area that will help you stay organized so you can stay on top of your progress and understand the appropriate next steps in your process. One of the reasons our methods are successful are as a direct result of the creditors and credit bureaus keeping poor records and violating the Fair Debt Collection Practices Act or Fair Credit Reporting Act. Our job is to help you point out these violations in a timely and effective manner so they know you are organized and serious — more often than not, they will elect to remove the negative items versus fighting you.

The methods we share are legal and effective. We encourage you to be honest with yourself, your creditors, and the credit bureaus throughout this process. This information should never be used to defraud a bank, make false claims, or purposefully default on a loan or financial obligation with hopes of using our techniques to remove the item later. These methods should be used to restore your credit and it is your responsibility to maintain your positive credit rating in the future.

Please only proceed if you agree to maintain integrity and conduct yourself in an ethical manner.

Errors on Credit Reports

Even an accurately reporting account could contain misinformation that is keeping your credit score down. A Public Interest Research Group (PIRG) study showed that 79% of credit reports contain detrimental errors. Scary, right?!? This book will show you how to identify those errors and remove unverifiable, inaccurate, or incomplete information from your report.

There are countless lawsuits and settlements that are publicly documented as a result of the credit bureaus failure to properly investigate and/or remove information from consumer credit reports. The dispute reinvestigation process came under fire during a recent FTC investigation. Under the Fair Credit Reporting Act the credit bureaus are required to conduct a reasonable investigation ("reinvestigation") and provide the methods used to verify information with the furnisher of the information. Often times, a dispute is processed using a software system called e-oscar which turns the dispute into a 2-digit code and uses automation to investigate a dispute. This automation is essentially a tool used to "cut corners", save time, and meet the 30-day deadline for reinvestigating a dispute and responding to you, the consumer.

I know what you're thinking, this is great information but when will you get to the part where you tell me how to get an 800 credit score!? I have to make sure you understand these few basic points so that you can fully comprehend the rest of the book and the methods and techniques we'll be using to challenge the items killing your score. The journey to the 700 club needs to be thought of as a marathon and not a sprint. There is no magic wand I can give you to instantly have perfect credit. But if you follow the tips and tricks in the book and follow along patiently with the course guide while utilizing the private Facebook community to talk to others dealing with similar issues —- you will be well on your way!

Your credit is not beyond repair. Feel encouraged and be proud of yourself for taking this all-important first step. Now all you have to do is follow this book, the course, and Facebook community and you'll be on your way to a better financial future. Many people have started following the techniques we share while their scores were in the low 400's —- they are now in the 700 Club! Today is the day you take control of your credit destiny and put the embarrassment (and high interest) of bad credit in your past once and for all.

Guilty Until Proven Innocent - A Backwards System

Our criminal justice system was founded on the premise of being innocent until proven guilty. However, when it comes to the data reflected on your credit report, you are presumed GUILTY until proven innocent. Tens of thousands of consumers are being turned down for home loans, credit cards, jobs, rental properties, and auto financing as a result of being convicted of a "crime" they may not have committed, and most are unaware of their legal right to fair and competent representation.

Criminal law requires the district attorney, prosecutors, and investigating officers to present a case and evidence to a jury of peers who must unanimously declare the guilt of the accused. Our credit reporting system works in a manner completely the opposite. Recent studies have shown that most credit reports contain serious errors. As these errors go unnoticed by the consumer, credit card companies are automatically increasing their interest rates, their car insurance premiums are going up, and auto finance companies and mortgage brokers are denying them access to financing. Consumers are left no choice but to accept the embarrassment of being denied credit and/or paying thousands of dollars in additional interest.

Correcting such errors requires the consumer to understand the consumer protection laws, credit scoring system, and dispute verification process. As it stands now, the consumer must prove to the credit bureaus that the account is reporting in error versus any accountability being placed on the credit bureaus and the creditors furnishing the outdated, erroneous, and unverifiable information. By definition, the consumer is GUILTY until proven innocent. Fighting for the consumer is precisely why I started The Credit Movement! With your financial future at stake, you deserve to understand the game. I will coach you on how to play the game — and play it well.

Your Credit is Not Beyond Repair

Many of our readers are embarrassed by the mistakes of their past. I'm here to tell you that your credit is not beyond repair. The fact that you are reading this book and have taken action indicates that you are motivated, and that is half the battle. Anytime you need a "pick-me-up", go to the Facebook Community and read about all the success others are having. You may be struggling today, but if you follow the steps outlined in this book, participate in the Facebook Community, and use the online courses — you too will be successful.

Jesse ▮▮▮▮ Thank you Ryan and your team. Your help and tips is helping me greatly into clearing my credit!
Like · Reply · Message · 🕐 1 · October 12 at 6:54pm

The Credit Movement You're very welcome, Jesse!
Like · Reply · Commented on by ▮▮▮▮ [?] · October 13 at 3:05am

Setting Your Goal

Before continuing with this book it is important that you set a goal. Whether you are starting with a 400 credit score or a 700, you need a goal to hit in order to set your intention for your journey and keep you focused and motivated. If you're just getting started working on your credit, your goal needs to be about taking small, achievable steps and hitting realistic milestones so you don't overcommit and get overwhelmed…if you do this, I guarantee you'll see results. If you are starting out with a 400 credit score, maybe your goal should be to get to a 640 credit score so you can qualify for a home loan and not pay astronomical interest rates on credit cards, auto loans, etc. While we all want to see that elusive 800 credit score, don't set a goal that could dishearten you. After you achieve your initial goal, keep raising the bar for yourself. Time is going to be your friend and not your enemy here, keeping a tight deadline is about staying focused so you're not letting unnecessary efforts get in the way of your progress. This is not about getting the perfect credit score, but rather getting you the best credit score for your unique set of circumstances. Now, if you haven't already, start writing down your goals. First, write down your credit score goal. Next, jot down your credit related goal (i.e. Buy a home for your family, buy that car you've always wanted, get an apartment, etc.). Now, write down the specific items you would like to address (i.e. Get rid of medical bills, deal with evictions, handle credit card debts, get a grip on student loans, etc.). I want to keep things moving so don't spend too much time on this step. I'm serious, I don't want you to spend more than 5 minutes on this. Set that goal, visualize yourself getting there, and lets get to work.

About Your Credit Movement Membership

I might be bias but feel it would be foolish for you to not take advantage of your FREE 30-day access to The Credit Movement Membership Area and the Exclusive Facebook Community. Remember, with the purchase of this book you will get 30 days of free access to the membership site which includes: A multitude of online courses that will help you with removing items that do not belong on your report. A private Facebook Community filled with many people embarking on a similar journey and sharing their successes. Access to a Document Vault chalked full of proven-effective letters you can use to challenge any item imaginable on your report, and much more.

The Private Facebook Page

I, personally, am involved in the exclusive Facebook Community, posting weekly videos and doing Facebook Live broadcasts to give everyone the opportunity to ask credit questions while I provide realtime answers. Join

13

this private community on Facebook by visiting https://facebook.com/groups/movementacademy.

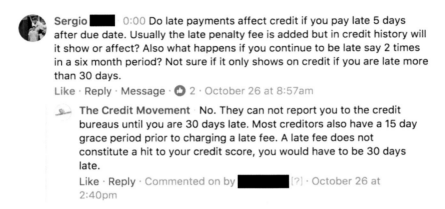

Many are waiting for you to introduce yourself. Once your access is approved be sure to say hello and use the hashtag: **#ReadyToRoll**

You will certainly feel like you have gotten to know me as the course is full of videos and tutorials within our online courses and on our Facebook page — that is why I would also like to know you. Be sure to get in the Facebook page and introduce yourself right away. Don't forget to use hashtag: **#ReadyToRoll**

We want the Facebook Community to be just that — a community. A place of positivity and motivation for all members. You will feel awesome for helping your friends in the community. When you have successes such as: items being deleted from your credit report, score increases, and/or approval for credit building accounts — use the hashtag: **#mymovement**

PLEASE NOTE: Because we want to protect the integrity of the private group, we only accept those that should be granted access to this exclusive page full of life-changing information — that being said, if your Facebook name does not match the name you used when purchasing our program please email us so we can approve you: **support@thecreditmovement.com**

Meet the Author - Ryan David

Ryan has one professional mission - "*To end credit and financial suffering for all*". Born and raised in a small fishing town in Wisconsin, Ryan learned the importance of dedication to helping others in his community. He found great joy in doing whatever possible to help others in need. After graduation from college, Ryan moved to Denver which is where he stumbled upon a career in consumer finance. He immediately became obsessed with our credit scoring system and its many faults. Very early on he decided to dedicate his professional career to learning everything there was to know about the many credit scoring algorithms and consumer protection laws. Once Ryan felt he knew more about the subject of consumer credit than most everyone in the country, he founded a company and began assisting thousands of consumers with ending their suffering. That extensive experience of facing every credit challenge imaginable — and conquering them, inspired Ryan to start The Credit Movement and condense his knowledge into this easy-to-understand book and guide to an empowered financial future. Ryan now lives in sunny Southern California with his wife Tara and their two daughters, Scarlett and Vivian.

Ryan David

Chapter 1:
Credit Reports and Scores

You DO NOT have just one universal credit score. It is important to understand that if you go to 100 different places you will likely get 100 different scores. Credit reports come in many shapes and sizes both in their appearance (layout) as well as with how the score is calculated.

Understanding FICO (Fair Isaac Company)

Did you know? There are multiple versions of the FICO score. While it is true that mortgage companies use FICO scores, it is important to understand which FICO scores they are using. Mortgage companies use FICO Classic 04, Fair Isaac V2, and FICO V5 FACTA. Banks, credit card companies, and car finance outlets often utilize a FICO score —- the FICO score they offer is much different from the mortgage score. For instance, they typically use FICO 8 or FICO 9. Car finance companies typically use what is called an "Industry Option FICO" which was designed by FICO specifically for car financing. The most common differences in these scores is the way they calculate and factor in medical debts and credit card utilization ratios.

FICO versus Consumer Scores (Credit Karma)

The multiple FICO score models vary greatly from the Vantage Score models being offered from online places such as Credit Karma and the like. They not only weigh the information on your report differently but also differ in the scoring scale. For instance, FICO Classic 04 may range from 331 to 843 while Vantage 3.0 ranges from

300 to 850. These are the reasons you get such different scores from different places.

You may also wonder why you get different scores between Experian, Equifax, and Transunion. That is most easily explained by the fact that not all things report to all 3 credit bureaus. You could have a collection that is only being reported to Transunion — your Transunion score in turn would be lower than your Experian and Equifax scores.

Getting your Credit Reports

In order to successfully understand, diagnose, and improve your credit rating, you must start by getting a copy of your credit report that reflects all 3 credit reporting agencies data. Many online providers such as Credit Karma only offer 2 of the 3 credit reporting agencies. Others offer just ONE.

The Credit Movement recommends our favorite source for credit reports which allows you the opportunity to get your reports from Experian, Equifax, AND Transunion! Better yet, you can monitor your credit and get updated reports monthly —- and it comes with a FREE TRIAL!

Ryan David

http://thecreditmovement.com/creditreport

A second option is http://AnnualCreditReport.com which offers all 3 reports for free once per year. You will not be given a score nor will you have the option to monitor your reports.

Components of the FICO Score

There are hundreds of algorithms out there for calculating credit scores. This is why when you go to Credit Karma your score is, for instance, 65 points higher than what a mortgage lender pulled up for you. Credit Karma uses something called a Vantage Score which is generated often times for general consumer purposes, i.e. online report providers. Mortgage companies must use approved algorithms that are determined by Fannie Mae and Freddie Mac or set mortgage lending criteria and guidelines. The algorithms, or score calculations, being used for mortgage purposes are currently; Experian - Fair Isaac V2, Equifax - FICO Classic V5 FACTA, Transunion - FICO Classic (04). Generally speaking the credit score ranges from approximately 300 to 850. Roughly, a 550 point scale. Continue to the next section to learn each section of your score.

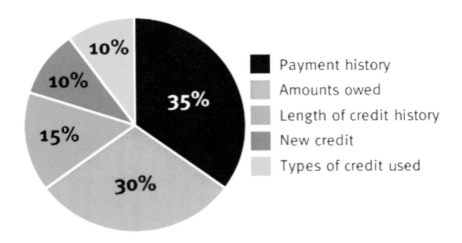

Legend:
- Payment history
- Amounts owed
- Length of credit history
- New credit
- Types of credit used

Pay Your Bills On-Time

35% - Payment History (Do you pay things on time?)

Paying your bills on time is the most obvious and important thing you can do for your credit. That being said, payment history has many layers to it. Many things other than 30, 60, 90, and 120-day late payments factor into the payment history section of your score.

Properly Manage Credit Card Utilization

30% - Credit Utilization on Revolving Accounts [credit cards] (Are you under 30%?)

Properly managing your credit cards and understanding the score exposure you face from a Home Equity Line of Credit ("HELOC") makes up the "revolving credit utilization" component of your score. The score calculator or algorithm penalizes those who carry a balance that is higher than 30% of their available credit limit. For instance, a $1000 credit limit would be ideal with a balance of less than $300. In my experience, paying down your credit card balances below the thresholds of 90%, 70%, 50%, and/or 30% of your limit will improve your score.

To help improve your balance-to-limit ratios on your credit cards, increase your limit to reduce utilization. Example: limit = $1000, balance = $900. If you increased the limit to $3,000, you would reduce the ratio of utilization from 90% to under 30%. Your score would likely increase significantly. As much as 60 points or more!

Considering a HELOC? Home Equity Line of Credit are dangerous to your credit report as a result of them being coded as a "revolving" account, or "R1" (if in good standing). I believe this is one of the bigger of the many failures of our credit scoring system. This "revolving credit utilization" portion of the score was designed to measure risk based on the consumer use of "unsecured" debt. Credit cards are more often than not, unsecured —

money borrowed with no real collateral. Despite the fact that HELOC's are secured by the property, they factor into the score the same way an unsecured credit card does. Often times, HELOC's are "interest only", meaning that unless you specifically make additional payments to the principle balance, your balance-to-limit ratio will always be at 100%. Obviously, this is extremely detrimental to your score. Later we will share tips and tricks to optimize your revolving debt balance-to-limit ratios.

Importance of Longer Credit History

15% - Length of Credit History (How long have you been in the credit game?)

The credit scoring system wants to know how long you have been in the credit game. The longer the better. An average of all your open credit accounts makes up your average length of credit history. Remember, this only factors in your OPEN accounts. Be careful not to close an old credit account that you have had open for a long time. Once it is closed, you will reduce your average length of credit history and potentially lower your score.

Importance of Credit Diversity

10% - Types of Credit (Do you have a good balance of accounts or only CC's?)

Having a good balance of credit accounts is a small but important portion of your credit score. There are 3 types of credit — Revolving, Installment, and Mortgage. It is ideal to have 3-8 revolving accounts as long as they are balanced with installment accounts such as an auto loan, student loan, or personal loan. Adding a mortgage gives the perfect balance of open/active/positive credit. If you are one of those consumers who opens up a store credit card every time you are offered 15% off your purchase - you may want to rethink your strategy. I once had a client who had 51 store credit cards…yikes!

The Truth About Inquiries

10% - New Credit (Did you open up a new account or get your credit pulled too much?)
Credit inquires and new accounts affects 10% of your overall credit score. It is imperative that you understand the impact that applying and opening new credit could have on your credit score. Especially if your short-term goal is to purchase a home. Opening up a new account could affect your credit score 15 points or more. The

algorithm used to calculate your credit score will penalize consumers for opening new credit, a method of deterring over-extending ones self. Shopping for a vehicle can be one of the most detrimental things you can do to your credit score. Car dealerships often tell you, "we are going to find you the best interest rate and lowest payment". What I have come to learn is that what they actually are doing is trying to find the highest kick-back. Car dealerships are entitled to what is often called a "bank fee". This is why the dealership will pull your credit 5, 10, or even 15 times or more — they are searching for who is going to pay them the most to give them the deal. See the below image showing 18 inquires over the course of 2 weekends of car shopping. This could hurt your credit score anywhere from 30 to 60 points!

Inquiries

Creditor Name	Date of inquiry	Credit Bureau
KOHLS/CAPONE	07/15/2016	TransUnion
RAY SKILLM	06/29/2016	Equifax
ALLYFINANC	06/29/2016	Equifax
CAP ONE AF	06/29/2016	Equifax
PRESTIGE	06/29/2016	Equifax
FRSTINVST	06/29/2016	Equifax
CAPITAL ONE AUTO FIN	06/29/2016	Experian
PRESTIGE FINANCIAL SVC	06/29/2016	Experian
FLAGSHIP CRE	06/29/2016	TransUnion
PRESTIGE FIN	06/29/2016	TransUnion
EXETER FIN	06/29/2016	TransUnion
CHASE AUTO	06/29/2016	TransUnion
COAF	06/29/2016	TransUnion
CHRYSLER CAP	06/29/2016	TransUnion
RSKILLMANAUT	06/29/2016	TransUnion
SYNCB	06/28/2016	Experian
RAY SKILLM	06/22/2016	Equifax
RSKILLMANAUT	06/22/2016	TransUnion
RAY SKILLM	06/21/2016	Equifax
CB/MEIJER	06/17/2016	Equifax

So what can you do to stop this? You have a few options — After you decided on a car, go to your local bank with the VIN number and agreed-upon purchase price and see if you can finance it with your bank directly. You could also visit a local credit union as they are typically willing to take on a loan when other large banks are reluctant. You could also request that the dealership only pulls your credit through one of their affiliate banks. Understanding the way car inquiries could damage your credit is important. You should also understand that there is a myth out there that consumers have a "30-day shopping window" and if your credit is being pulled for the same purpose (i.e. auto loan, home loan, credit card) that it only counts as one inquiry. This is only true if the inquiries are coded the same way and pulled through the same provider. Auto finance companies will code inquiries as "consumer", "auto loan", "auto lease", etc. Each of these types would hurt your score 3-5 points for the first 6 months with a diminishing impact over time.

Inquiries remain on your report for up to 2 years. There are 3 types of inquiries: hard, soft, and promotional. The hard inquiries are of the utmost importance as these are the ones that, as just mentioned, ding your score 3-5 points for the first 6 months with a diminishing impact over the 2 year period they remain. Hard inquiries happen anytime you apply for something — a home loan, an auto loan, a credit card, etc. Pulling your own credit as a consumer does not negatively impact your score. These are considered soft inquires. Another form of a soft inquiry is known as an "Account Review Inquiry". Typically these are done by credit card companies to reassess risk. For instance, if your score goes down 40 points, the credit card company reserves the right to increase your interest. Another travesty of the credit scoring system is that during one of these routine credit checks if your score happens to go up, they will not lower your interest rate.

Promotional inquiries are a form of acquiring data for direct mail or other forms of marketing credit cards or services to a consumer.

The credit bureaus, Experian, Equifax, and Transunion are not private companies but rather for-profit, publicly traded entities. They have a duty to make money for their shareholders and one of the ways they do that is by selling consumer data to anyone willing to purchase it. An example would be Capital One wanting to market a credit card to consumers via a direct-mail campaign of "pre-approval" letters. They contact Equifax and say we will give $150,000 for a list of 1 million consumers with credit scores ranging from say, 620-660. They target a specific group of consumers that their research indicates pay their bills on time, but is somewhat irresponsible with their credit decisions. This is exactly what the credit card companies want — an individual who has a high probability, according to their research, of getting approved for a $2000 limit credit card, and then proceeds to max it out and then make minimum payments for the rest of their life at 19% interest or even more. Jackpot for the credit card company.

Chapter 2:
Reading Your Report
(Getting Ready for Battle)

Improving your credit report is impossible if you don't even know what you are looking for. It's also important that you learn to identify common errors and opportunities to improve your score. If you don't yet have a copy of your report it is important that you get a copy before continuing.

Credit Karma and other free online credit reports are great, however, they do not contain account numbers.

We will need a report that contains all the pertinent information needed to begin cleaning things up.
http://thecreditmovement.com/creditreport

We recommend this report because it comes with a free trial. You can elect to cancel within the trial period or keep it going while working through our book and online courses. Keeping your account open will allow you to monitor the progress and pull new reports as needed to track disputes.

While there are many different formats of credit reports they are typically not too difficult to read once you familiarize yourself. In this chapter we will take a look at some reports so you can confidently go through your report and identify all possible opportunities to improve your score! We will take some immediate action on personal information discrepancies. We will also learn to identify other detrimental and derogatory items that we will provide letters for challenging in the later chapters.

Removing unauthorized or unrecognizable inquiries is an important step in the process to optimizing your credit. Remember, an inquiry could hurt you up to 5 points. The following letters will help you remove the inquiries that do not belong on your report.

Now that you have your report, lets learn to read it and find all the opportunities to clean it up! If you don't yet have your report, now is the time to get it. http://thecreditmovement.com/creditreport

Personal Information

At the top of your report you'll see the personal information section which includes your name and aliases, mailing address history, social security number, date of birth, and employer history. It is important to document any incorrect names/aliases, social security numbers, dates of birth, employer data, and mailing addresses. Understand that each address is given an "address identification number" — each trade line on your report is associated with one of those address identifiers. Removing unnecessary addresses will allow a pathway to removing accounts later that do not belong on your report. Available through our website, **http://TheCreditMovement.com** is a course titled "Free Mini Course" which walks you through, in detail, correcting personal information. We will walk you through it here as well. Go through your report and document any inaccurate personal information. Be sure to include all previous and inaccurate addresses.

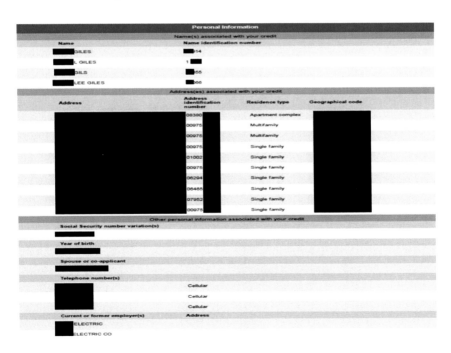

Ryan David

How and Where to Send Dispute Letters

Anytime you send dispute letters to the credit bureaus it is important that you send them Certified Mail with Return Receipt. Create a paper trail and keep records of what, where, and when you send letters. It is not necessary to sign the letters you send to the credit bureaus. Include with the letter a copy of your drivers license, social security card, and a recent utility bill verifying your mailing address. Let's prepare and send our first letter to the credit bureaus! Please note: By law, the credit bureaus have 30 days to respond to disputes. You are likely to start receiving correspondences in the mail within 3-4 weeks from the time you send the letters.

Inquiry Removal Letter 1

(Set of 2 - One to Bureaus, One to Creditors directly)

Remember to replace all of the red text with your information in black.

You may get a letter from Experian stating "We received a suspicious request…", ignore this letter. As long as you sent a copy of your driver's license, social security card, and a utility bill —- they will respond. If the items get deleted —- Congratulations. If they do not, proceed with "Inquiry Removal Letter 2".

Your Name
Your Address
Creditor Name
Creditor Address
Date

Re: Unauthorized Credit Inquiry

To Whom It May Concern,

A recent review of my credit report showed an unauthorized credit inquiry from your company. I understand that, by law, you are not able to place an inquiry on my credit report without my prior authorization and signature. Please have this inquiry removed from my credit file immediately as it is causing me great financial hardship and limiting my purchasing power.

I have sent this letter via certified mail as I need prompt attention to this matter. Kindly forward me your confirmation of the removal of this unauthorized inquiry.

If you find that I am mistaken, and you do have my authorization to inquire into my credit report, then please send me proof of this. Include my signature on your authorization form. Otherwise, please note that I am reserving the right to take civil action if necessary. I also will notify the CFPB, FTC, and Attorney General if necessary.

Thank you,

Your Name (printed or typed, not signed)

Inquiry Removal Letter 2

In the event you receive a letter stating the accounts were "verified", send this!

Ryan David

Your Name
Your Address
Credit Bureau Name
Credit Bureau Address
Date
RE: Social Security Number: 000-00-0000

To Whom It May Concern,

I am deeply troubled by the fact that I noticed credit inquiries on my report maintained by your company that I did not authorize. Please immediately remove the below unauthorized inquires.

Unauthorized Inquiries:
1. (insert company name & inquiry date)
2. (insert company name & inquiry date)
3. (insert company name & inquiry date)

This is a violation of the Fair Credit Reporting Act Section 1681b(c) and a serious breach of my privacy rights. I did not authorize anyone at any of these to make any inquiry into my credit report.

If for some reason you validate this information with these companies, please provide me with copies of any documentation associated with these accounts bearing my signature which would constitute an authorized inquiry. If you are unable to obtain documentation bearing my signature, I formally request that these fraudulent inquiries be immediately deleted from the credit file that you maintain.

Under the Fair Credit Reporting Act section 611, you have 30 days to complete this request.

My contact information is as follows:

Your Name (printed or typed, not signed)
SSN
Address

These are the first two of many letters we will be sharing in this book. The free online mini course available on our member site also will hold your hand through inquiry removal techniques.

Removing Outdated and Incorrect Mailing Addresses

Let's remove those outdated and incorrect mailing addresses. Use this letter and be sure to fill in all of the areas in Red with your information. Also, always include a copy of your driver's license, social security card, and two recent utility bills that verifies your mailing address.

It is not necessary to sign the letters and ALWAYS send them certified mail with return receipt. Please note that a step-by-step guide including a downloadable version of this and all letters is available through the courses in The Credit Movement member site.

Date

Credit Bureau Name
Credit Bureau Address

To Whom It May Concern:

I am writing to correct inaccurate personal information on my credit report with your company.

Please update my address to:

[Insert Address]

Please remove all the other addresses o my report, as they are not deliverable to me by the U.S. post office, and they are not reportable as per the FCRA, since they are inaccurate.

Sincerely,

Name

{Signature}

Enclose: Driver License, SSN Card, and Proof of Residence (Utility Bill)

Removing inaccurate and outdated mailing addresses is a key step. Now that you have covered that, you need to correct: names/aliases, incorrect social security numbers, dates of birth, and employer history.

Correcting Inaccurate Names, Social Security Numbers, Dates of Birth, and Employer History

Having incorrect personal information on your report may lead to having accounts that do not belong on your report, potentially lowering your score. Most readers will NOT find errors in their social security number and date of birth. If you do, it's a must you correct them as soon as possible. This letter should be customized by you to include the information you wish to correct.

Date

Credit Bureau Name
Credit Bureau Address

To Whom It May Concern:

I am writing to request an update to my personal information on file with your company.

Please update my [Social / Date of Birth / Employer History / Names and Aliases] **to:**

[Insert Correct Information Here]

Please remove all the other [Insert Necessary Wording - Social / Date of Birth / Employer History / Names and Aliases] my report, as they are not deliverable to me by the U.S. post office, and they are not reportable as per the FCRA, since they are inaccurate.

Sincerely,

Name

{Signature}

Enclosed: Driver License, SSN Card, and Proof of Residence (Utility Bill)

Reading Accounts on your Credit Report

Following the personal information section you get into the trade lines that are being reported to the credit bureaus. These trade line items ultimately factor into your score. When scanning the trade lines it is important to notice the account type, account status, and payment history. Notice account types such as Charge off, Included in Bankruptcy, Profit and Loss, and Collection. The below image gives you an idea of what to look for.

Notice the "Charged Off" status and "Bankruptcy" note in the remarks. Check for duplicate accounts. Here is an example: Capital One credit card went unpaid and was charged off, after writing off the account as a loss on their books (taxes), they then sold it to ABC Collections — now the same account is on your report multiple times.

Look for glaring errors that give you a solid reason for disputing and requesting removal. Some errors are more obvious than others. You are the best judge of accuracy of information on your report. You know what items are legitimate. You know who you authorized to pull your credit. You know whether or not a certain account should show as included in a bankruptcy. You know if that medical bill should have been covered by insurance. Be sure to write down all items you would like to dispute so we may challenge them in the next chapter.

The image below shows an obvious error — a collection account showing a "Last Reported Date" of November 25, 2015. The "Opened Date" is March 18, 2017.

Now, I'm no rocket scientist, but, if the account was opened in March of 2017, how can it be last reported to the credit bureaus in November of 2015?! This needs to be disputed based on the conflicting dates being reported.

Collections

Account Details

Last Reported	Nov 25, 2015
Collection Agency	
Original Creditor	TIME WARNER CABLE
Status	Open
Opened Date	Mar 18, 2017
Closed Date	--
Responsibility	Individual Account.
Balance	--
High Balance	--
Remarks	Bankruptcy chapter 7 Bankruptcy discharged

Be sure to make note of the balance reporting for each charge off, profit and loss, and collection. It's important to point out that the algorithm doesn't distinguish between paid and unpaid collections. For example, a $10,000 balance on an open collection could impact your score in the same way as a collection with a $0 balance. I know, it sounds crazy, but it's true. If the original creditor data is available, be sure to document that so we may challenge it in the next chapter. Each of these steps are important. Because of HIPAA privacy laws, medical debts often leave off the name of the hospital or clinic where the medical debt originated — that is ok, just note original creditor as "medical". If you have a collection for ABC Collections, for instance, and it notes the original credit as XYZ Apartment Property Management — this would indicate an "eviction" and it's important it is documented as such so you can work to correct it using the appropriate steps in the chapters. Later we'll discuss how to deal with each of these accounts!

Late Payments and Payment History

You also want to scan your report and search the payment history on all active and closed accounts. Account statuses showing as delinquent, past due, or current/previously late and showing 30/60/90/120+ day late payments are one of the most damaging items to your credit report and score, especially if they are recent. Late payments on closed and/or paid off accounts still impacts your score negatively.

Late payments on student loans can be particularly troublesome. Many readers have multiple student loans as a result of the process for obtaining them. Each semester, typically, you fill out your Financial Aid paperwork and loan forms. At the end of 2 years of college you would then have 4 accounts — one for each semester. Once you are finished with school and deferment/forbearance is over, you start repayment. Most people consolidate or make one payment. If you happen to miss a payment, you will show a 30-day late payment on 4 accounts (or 8 if you did 4 years of school). These must be challenged! Be sure to make note of any questionable late payments so we may challenge them in the next chapter.

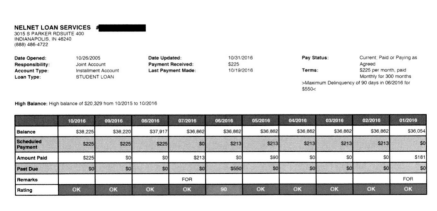

Even accurately reported late payments can be challenged using a technique called a "Goodwill Letter" which will be discussed later. Notice the late payment in the below image.

Identifying Public Records

Public records can be found either at the top of your report before the trade line information begins, or after the trade line information nearer the bottom of the report. The section will be labeled as "Public Record" and will include: Bankruptcies, Judgements, and State and Federal Tax Liens. In July 2017, the credit bureaus made public that as a result of many inaccuracies in reporting, they will no longer report many judgement and tax lien accounts. Lets hope you're one of the lucky ones!

Bankruptcy can be one of the most inaccurately reported items on a consumer credit report. All too often, accounts on the credit report do not match the accounts on the court discharge paperwork. The bankruptcy trustee often does not update the credit bureaus as to which accounts were officially discharged through the bankruptcy. Because these accounts are often inaccurately reported, you must dispute them for removal. You can also frame an argument for removal of the bankruptcy public record itself. Note any questionable public records so we may dispute them in the upcoming chapters!

DID YOU KNOW? Collection agencies often have multiple call centers. Knowing this helps you because if you are requesting a "letter of deletion" over the phone while calling the collection agency — if at first you don't succeed...dust yourself off and try again. Many in our community have used this technique and had great success. If the first call center states they do not offer a "letter of deletion", Google the collection agency's customer service phone number and call and request a one-time courtesy letter of deletion from the alternative call center.

Identifying Your Bad Credit Items to Dispute

Please note: You have the legal right to challenge anything you would like to question on your report. In the upcoming chapter we will begin disputing actual trade line items that could be considered inaccurate, obsolete, outdated, incomplete, or unverifiable. Be sure you have written down the account name and account number from your credit report for all items you would like to challenge for removal. This can include: Judgements, Collections, Evictions, Repossessions, Bankruptcies, Late Payments, Credit Card Information, etc.

IMPORTANT TO REMEMBER: Easy to follow step-by-step courses are available through our member site in the event the book method for challenging items does not work for you. The letters are downloadable in an editable version and video tutorials will guide you through dealing with specific issues.

Throughout this book you are given techniques for challenging questionable items. Many readers have asked if we would recommend calling or faxing to challenge items — in short, the answer is no. In our years of experience the most effective method is to send certified mail to the creditors and/or credit bureaus. This does a number of things that are beneficial to you when initiating a challenge. It creates a paper trail. It encourages human interaction versus a 2-digit code filtered through a software called e-oscar. Some online disputes even include a disclaimer waiving your right to challenge an item again if you are given an unfavorable response.

Many also ask about doing online disputes offered through Credit Karma and other online credit report sites. Again, this is not recommended as it allows the bureaus and creditors to communicate regarding the dispute using a software program and is not as effective as formal investigations issued using certified mail.

Chapter 3:
Disputing Items for Removal
(The Good Stuff)

You have the legal right to challenge any item reporting on your credit report. The burden of proof is on the credit bureaus to validate what they are reporting is accurate —it is not on you to prove that they are reporting inaccurately. That is an important fact to keep in mind as you continue your journey to better credit.

Original creditor and collection agency practices for attempting to collect on a debt are governed by the Fair Debt Collection Practices Act and the Fair Credit Reporting Act — among other related consumer protection laws. The laws below are the specific consumer protection laws that Experian, Equifax, Transunion, and the creditors must abide by.

Fair Credit Reporting Act (FCRA)

The Fair Credit Reporting Act clearly states that items on a consumer credit report must be reporting with completeness, accuracy, and verifiability. According to a recent study, 79% of credit reports contain detrimental errors. Obsolete information must be properly disputed for removal at a credit bureau level. Later we will share sample dispute letters and include specific language of the FCRA, mainly focused on Section 623.

Fair Debt Collections Practices Act (FDCPA)

The Fair Debt Collection Practices Act contains laws that outline the guidelines that must be followed by collection agencies that are attempting to collect money from you. Later you will notice in the sample letters that we focus on Section 807 of the FDCPA.

Most Common Creditor Violations:
1. Discuss your alleged debt with a third party (employer or friend, etc.)
2. Give misleading information regarding the amount you owe
3. Call you before 8am or after 9pm (your time, not theirs)
4. Misrepresent information regarding the alleged debt to a credit bureau
5. Threaten you with wage garnishments or selling your property

Reasons for Dispute:
Here are some of the reasons for challenging an account:
- Incorrect balance

- Not your account
- Inaccurate "Status"
- Missing or incorrect dates
- Never paid late
- Account outside statute of limitations
- Incorrect or missing limit
- Actual balance lower than high balance
- Late payments showing after account closed
- Inaccurate account open date
- Inaccurate date of 1st delinquency
- Incomplete or inaccurate account number
- Date of last activity inaccurate (this date is important as it is used to determine when the 7 year statute of limitations begins)
- Incorrect account type
- Charge off listed as open account or collection status
- Late payments showing on collection
- Limit showing on a collection account (not possible)

Important Rules to Follow When Sending Letters

Sending dispute letters to your creditors and the credit bureaus is a big part of the process of improving your credit score. The below important rules should always be followed. These rules are designed to improve your chances of a favorable result. If you do not follow these rules you are likely to encounter headaches. You will likely get stall tactic form letters from the credit bureaus. Your letters may be altogether rejected. You may cause more harm than good. Follow these rules!

All mail being sent to the credit bureaus and/or creditors should be sent certified mail with return receipt. It is important that we create a paper trail and keep detailed records of when and where things were mailed. On day 31 following them signing for your letter, print out a copy of your report —if the bureaus are not showing the account in dispute, they have violated the Fair Credit Reporting Act and you now have leverage

Always include a copy of your Drivers License, Social Security Card, AND a piece of mail that verifies your mailing address. A utility bill typically works well

For the Mailing Address dispute letters; include all above and ONE additional piece of mail. (Two total pieces of mail)

Always fill in any sections in Red on the dispute sample letters provided in the course

The Personal Information letter includes [Social Security # / Date of Birth / Employer History / Names and Aliases]. In the event you need to correct more than one of these items include multiple correction requests in this letter

Credit Bureau Mailing Addresses:

Equifax
P.O. Box 7404256
Atlanta, GA 30374-0256

Experian
Dispute Department
P.O. Box 9701
Allen, TX 75013

TransUnion
Consumer Solutions
P.O. Box 2000
Chester, PA 19022-2000

For direct-to-creditor letters you will need to find the mailing addresses for those companies. These addresses can typically be found on the credit report either within the account information itself, or at the end of the report

It is not necessary to put your signature on a dispute letter

Did you know? When it comes to impact on your score, there is no difference between a paid collection with a $0 balance and one with a $1,000,000 balance.

A collection's negative impact on your score is measured within the algorithm by looking at the way the account is coded and the "date of last activity". An account coded as "O-9" or "I-9" or "R-9" would indicate a collection or charge off type of account to the score calculator (algorithm). Once the score calculator knows there is a collection, the next thing they want to know is, 'how much should this collection hurt the score?' —this is where the date of last activity comes into play. The more recent the date of last activity, the more it hurts the score. How does the date of last activity get reset, you ask? — By you making a payment. So, yes, paying a collection hurts your score! It's not a fair system. We always recommend making sure a debt is validated prior to even considering paying it. If it can't be validated it must be removed. If it is valid, if possible, offer payment in full in exchange for a letter of deletion. We'll talk more about this later.

Also factoring into payment history is old accounts that are now paid off but have old late payments or derogatory history. Simply having a $0 balance on an account does not mean that account's history is not negatively impacting the score. We will also be discussing how to work to remove these accounts later. Public Records such as Bankruptcy, Tax Liens, and Judgements also negatively impact the payment history section of the score. Recent changes in credit scoring eliminated the reporting of much of the tax lien and judgement data to the credit bureaus.

Bankruptcies are commonly misreported on credit reports. For instance, your chapter 7 was discharged and included 27 accounts, yet your credit report shows 17 accounts as open/active charge off or collection accounts. Only 10 are properly reported as included in bankruptcy. Our online courses walk you through the process of identifying and challenging specific accounts for removal.

The Responses You Will Receive from the Letters

The letters and dispute techniques we are about to share will result in you receiving correspondences in the mail from the credit bureaus and creditors. It is important that you maintain records of what you sent, when you sent it, and what you received in return. If at any point you have questions regarding things you receive in the mail you have a community here to help you. Our Facebook Community will help you — get in there and ask your question! If you're not using the community simply email **support@TheCreditMovement.com**.

The results you receive will determine the next step as you will find out soon. Here is a sampling of what you're likely to receive in the mail as a result of sending the letters.

Experian "Suspicious Request" Letter

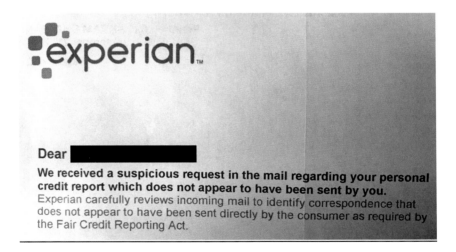

Most readers who take action will receive this letter. This is simply a stall tactic form letter. Resend your original letter with enclosed documents (Drivers License, Social, Utility bill) and include a copy of the "suspicious request" letter. You will then receive the required investigation results.

Transunion Results

Below you can see the results of the Transunion Results.

Equifax Results

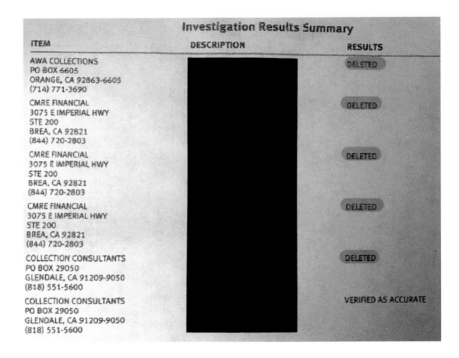

Below you can see the Equifax Results with arrows pointing to the important part, "deleted". Notice a few of the accounts are "verified". We will cover the Method of Verification ("MOV") letter later in the chapter.

If interested, you may also request a description of how the reinvestigation was conducted along with the business name, address and telephone number (if reasonably available) of the furnisher of information.

Thank you for helping ensure the accuracy of your credit information.

For frequently asked questions about your credit report, please visit experian.com/consumerfaqs.

If no information follows, our response appeared on the previous page.

By law, we cannot disclose certain medical information (relating to physical, mental, or behavioral health or condition). Although we do not generally collect such information, it could appear in the name of a data furnisher (e.g. "Cancer Center") that reports your payment history to us. If so, those names display on your report, but on reports to others, they display only as MEDICAL PAYMENT DATA. Consumer statements included on your report at your request that contain medical information are disclosed to others.

Results

We have completed the processing of your dispute(s). Here are the results:

Credit items

MED-1 SOLUTIONS ███████ ✓
Outcome: Deleted - This item was removed from your credit report. Please review your report for the details.

TRANSWORLD SYS INC ███ ████████ ✓
Outcome: Deleted - This item was removed from your credit report. Please review your report for the details.

CREDIT PROTECTION ASSO ████████ ✓
Outcome: Deleted - This item was removed from your credit report. Please review your report for the details.

Visit experian.com/status to check the status of your pending disputes at any time.

Experian Results After you have combatted the "suspicious request" letter you will receive results from Experian that appear similar to what you see below. Please note that on rare occasions, the credit bureaus will simply NOT respond at all. Later in the chapter we will advise on what letter to send if you just flat out get no response from one of the credit bureaus.

Creditor Verification Letter

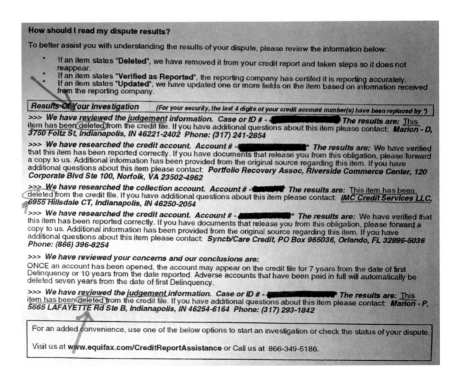

The Credit Movement

It is not uncommon for a creditor to respond directly to you. This often happens even if you did not send them a letter and only sent letters to the bureaus. This is commonly referred to as a verification letter. They are verifying the accuracy of the debt. You can later send the MOV letter to the credit bureaus.

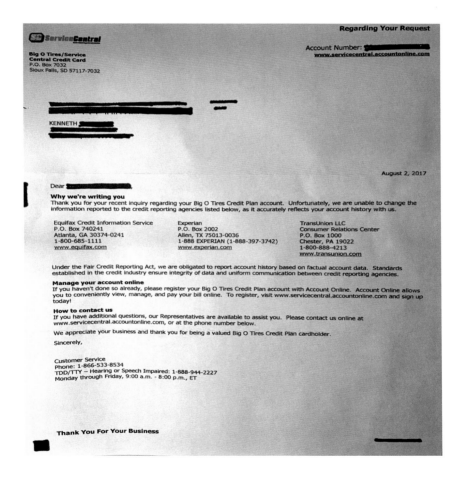

Creditor Deletion Letter

Not to be confused with a "letter of deletion" discussed later in the advanced techniques section, the creditor deletion letter comes as a result of a dispute letter being sent. This is a favorable outcome and no further action is required.

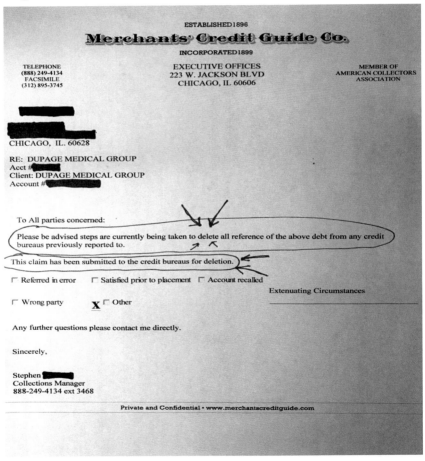

The Letters and Dispute Techniques

Always remember to send the letters certified mail with return receipt requested. This is important so that you can start the clock on the day they sign. Having and monitoring your credit report is very important at this stage. If you do not yet have a report from all 3 bureaus that included all account information and account numbers, go here now!
http://thecreditmovement.com/creditreport

Mark your calendar to check your credit report on day 31 from date they signed. If the account is not listed as "in dispute" or "consumer disputes" you need to immediately print your report. Be sure the date and time stamp is on the credit report. The credit bureaus are only allowed 30 days by law to investigate your dispute. You now have ammunition that can be used against them for violating the FDCPA and FCRA. Remember, the credit scoring system consider you guilty until proven innocent. That being said, the burden of proof is on the credit bureaus to prove they are reporting complete, accurate, and verifiable information. You have the legal right to challenge any information on your report.

Just because an account is yours that does not mean it is reporting accurately. The account could be:

* Duplicated
* Missing or incorrect balance
* Incorrect date
* Inaccurate credit limit
* Invalid or Incorrect Status
* Inaccurate late payment
* Incorrect date of first delinquency

Letters - Group 1 (Challenging Accounts for Removal)

Remember that with the purchase of this book you are granted 30 days of free access to our Online Course, Facebook Community, and Membership site. While we can't include EVERY letter in this book, we do have an online course with over 50 different sample dispute letters.

The letters in group 1 should be used as initial letters to challenge erroneous, derogatory, and/or collection accounts. Use these only for accounts you wish to be removed from your credit report permanently. Prepare and draft these letters as soon as possible.

Letter 1.1 (Creditor Initial Dispute)

Send directly to bank or agency that is reporting to the credit bureaus the obsolete or inaccurate derogatory account or collection item. This letter will use legal language from FDCPA Section 807.

Date
Your Name
Your Address
Name of creditor/collection agency
Address of creditor/collection agency (from your credit report)
Re: Acct # 123456789

To Whom It May Concern:

This letter is in regards to account #123456789, which you claim [insert a derogatory condition here, such as "I owe $150" or "that my account was charged off in the amount of $375]. Allow this notice to serve as a formal dispute of your claim.

Ryan David

Since I am quite familiar with my rights under the Fair Debt Collection Practices Act (FDCPA), the Fair Credit Reporting (FCRA), as well as state laws — I am requesting validation of this alleged account. Pursuant to the aforementioned laws, I am requesting that evidence **bearing my signature** be provided as required by law, proving my current or prior contractual obligation to pay you for this alleged account.

Under the FDCPA and FCRA, if you, or any company you represent, are unable to validate any debt that you claim that I owe, you are in violation of the law. Therefore, if you fail to validate the debt, I am requesting that you uphold your legally required duty and request that all credit reporting agencies (Experian, Equifax, Transunion, Innovis, LexisNexis) delete the account.

Depending on your response to this formal request, I am prepared to detail my experience via a public press release online. I will also include documentation of any potential small claims action. A complaint will also be filed with the Consumer Financial Protection Bureau (CFPB), Office of the Attorney General (OAG), and the Better Business Bureau (BBB).

Pending the outcome of my investigation and any evidence you submit, you are formally instructed to take no further action that could be detrimental to my credit rating or credit reports.

This letter is written as a formal request to correct your records and reporting to the credit bureaus. This request is for information only and is not a statement, waiver of status, or election — of any kind. Let it be known that any correspondences received from your company will be stored as evidence should any further action be required to resolve the matter in question.

By law, a response to this inquiry is required no later than 30 days from receipt of this certified letter. In the event you fail to comply, legal action in the form of small claims against your company may be filed in my local jurisdiction — seeking a minimum of $1,000 in damages per violation, including but not limited to:

* FCRA Violations of Section 623-b
* FDCPA Violations of 807-8
* Defamation
* Negligent Enablement of Identity Fraud

Ryan David

My contact information is as follows:

Your Name (printed, no signature)
Your Mailing Address

Cc: CFPB
Cc: OAG
Cc: BBB

Letter 1.2 (Bureau Initial Dispute)

This is your initial dispute or investigation request to be sent to the credit bureaus. This letter will focus on FCRA Section 611.

Your Name
Your Address
Credit Bureau Name
Credit Bureau Address
Date
RE: Social Security Number: 000-00-0000

To Whom It May Concern:

It has come to my attention during a recent review of the credit report in my name and social security number maintained by your company, that negative information is being reported by [Insert Creditor Name/Collection Agency/Public Record Court Name].

The account in question is showing that [insert a derogatory condition here, such as "I owe $150" or "that my account was charged off in the amount of $375]. This account is showing as last reported on [insert month and year].

Allow this letter to serve as a formal challenge as to your legal capacity to report the aforementioned account. I am requesting the immediate deletion of this account from my credit report. In the event you elect not to fulfill my request for immediate deletion of the account, I request for you to provide me with documentation *bearing my signature* from [Insert Creditor Name/Collection Agency/Public Record Court Name].

The Fair Credit Reporting Act Section 611 (a)(1)(A) allows 30 days for you to respond and provide your specific Method of Verification (MOV). Please note that any correspondences from your company, including your MOV will be stored as evidence in the event further action is necessary to resolve this matter.

Ryan David

Furthermore, I do not consent to any automated methods of verification, including that of the software, e-oscar.

By law, a response to this inquiry is required no later than 30 days from receipt of this certified letter. In the event you fail to comply, legal action in the form of small claims against your company may be filed in my local jurisdiction — seeking a minimum of $1,000 in damages per violation, including but not limited to:

* FCRA Violations
* Negligent Enablement of Identity Fraud
* Defamation

An online review and press release along with complaints to the Consumer Financial Protection Bureau (CFPB), Office of Attorney General (OAG), and Better Business Bureau (BBB) may be filed depending on your response to this request.

Please find my contact information below:

Your Name (printed, no signature required)

Your Mailing Address

Cc: CFPB

Cc: OAG

Cc: BBB

Enclosures: Copy of Drivers License, Social Security Card, Utility Bill (Proof of Mailing Address)

Letter 1.3 (Creditor Goodwill Letter)

This letter can be used for that rare late payment or two. Many readers will have account with favorable payment history, but due to an oversight, illness, or other unforeseen circumstance — they missed a payment resulting in a 30 day late payment being recorded with the credit bureaus. Often times creditors will take reasonable consideration and do a courtesy removal of those rare late payments. Use this letter in those instances.

Your Name
Your Address
Creditor Name
Creditor Address

Ryan David

Date
RE: Account # 123456789

To Whom It May Concern,

I'm writing out of concern for a late payment I noticed when viewing my credit report. The late payment in question was reported on [insert month(s)]_for my [insert company name]_account. For your convenience, that account number is [insert account number].

At the time of the aforementioned missed payment, I had [insert reason for late payment – overseas travel, medical incident, loss of income, extended hospital stay, debilitating injury, etc]. As you can see, I brought the account current as soon as I possibly could, and with the exception of this rare occurrence, have and will remain current on all payments.

In the not-so-distant future, I intend to [insert reason - apply for a home loan, apply for an auto loan, apply for student loan for my son/daughter], and I am well aware of the impact this unintentional late payment will have on my ability to attain financing.

I fully understand that my credit report and score is an indication of my ability to pay back a loan and the risk associated with lending me money. With this rare late payment showing on my credit report, I do not feel that my credit score reflects my true ability to fulfill my ability to pay.

For that reason, I am kindly requesting a one-time courtesy removal of the late payment from [insert month(s)] on my [insert company name] account.

For your consideration, and on behalf of my family, I thank you from the bottom of my heart.

It is worth notifying you that I take my financial responsibilities seriously and have every intention of fulfilling my financial obligation to your company and will remain timely in doing so.

Thank you for your consideration.
Make it a Great Day!

Kindest Regards,
Your Name (Printed, no signature)
Your Address

Letters - Group 2 (Follow up Action)

Letter 2.1 (Creditor Method of Verification)

Send this letter if you receive a response to "Letter 1.1" that your account was verified or accurate.

Date
Your Name
Your Address
Name of creditor/collection agency
Address of creditor/collection agency (from your credit report)

Re: Acct # 123456789

To Whom It May Concern:

This letter is in response to your recent claim regarding account # 123456789, which you claim [Insert Creditor Name/Collection Agency/Public Record Court Name].

Not surprisingly, I have NOT received evidence **bearing my signature** which would serve as proof of the above referenced account being reported accurately.

Let this serve as confirmation that your explanation and description of procedures used to reach your conclusion are documented as evidence in my ongoing quest for justice.

Your inability to provide ample evidence of the procedures and methods used to determine the accuracy and completeness of the information in question is also sufficiently documented.

I am requesting to be provided with the following information for each individual who verified this alleged account:

* Full Name
* Mailing Address
* Telephone Number
*

This provided information will be used to inquire on specifically how they "verified" without provided the previously requested evidence *bearing my signature.*

Per a Federal Trade Commission opinion letter a simple printout of a bill or even an itemized document does not qualify as "verification". The opinion letter can be found

here
http://educationcenter2000.com/debt_collectors/FT
C%20opinion%20letter%20on%20validation%20Sec
tion%20809(a)%20of%20the%20FDCPA.htm

Please immediately provide the previously requested evidence *bearing my signature*, or DELETE this account at once as it is clear there is no proof or binding obligation between myself and the alleged account.

It goes without saying that I will continue to keep diligent records of all communications and correspondences and if this final attempt goes unresolved I will be filing formal complaints immediately with the agencies cc'd on this communication.

Your non-compliance with the FCRA and FDCPA exposes you to damages for such violations. I will seek a minimum of $1,000 in damages for each violation. Small claims would be filed for:

*Defamation

*Violating the Fair Debt Collection Practices Act, particularly Section 807-8.

* Violating the Fair Credit Reporting Act, particularly Section 623-B

* Negligent Enablement of Identity Fraud

The court is likely to request your presence in my local jurisdiction.

Your Name (typed, no signature required)
Your Mailing Address
Social Security #

Cc: Consumer Financial Protection Bureau
Cc: Attorney General's Office
Cc: Better Business Bureau

Letter 2.2 (Creditor Failure to Respond in legally required time)

Use this letter if the creditor did not respond to "Letter 1.1".

Date
Your Name
Your Address
Name of creditor/collection agency
Address of creditor/collection agency (from your credit report)
Re: Acct # 123456789

To Whom It May Concern:

Ryan David

This letter is in reference to a claim by your company regarding account #123456789.

It appears that your are claiming [insert a derogatory condition here, such as "I owe $150" or "that my account was charged off in the amount of $375]

The law requires a timely response to any request for information or investigation. Since you failed to not only reply, but to provide ample evidence **_bearing my signature_**, you are in clear violation of the federal and state laws put into place to protect consumers.

My original letter for which you neglected to respond was sent on [Insert Date you sent the letter]

This will be my final attempt to have you resolve this blatantly obvious error in reporting on your behalf.

For my own protection, I am tracking and documenting all communications regarding this issue. In the event this final goodwill request for compliance is unsuccessful, I will be left no choice but to pursue this matter further, exhausting all available resources to come to a just resolution. This includes filing a formal complaint with the Consumer Financial

Protection Bureau, Office of the Attorney General, and Better Business Bureau, among other public online press releases sharing my experience.

I also remind you of your legal exposure with respect to non-compliance.

Failure to produce a copy of any supposed binding contract which bears my signature may result in small claims against your company.

As seems to be customary with these types of claims, I would be seeking a minimum of $1,000 in damages per violation for:

· Defamation
· Negligent Enablement of Identity Fraud
· Violating the Fair Debt Collection Practices Act (particularly Section 807-8)
· Violating the Fair Credit Reporting Act (particularly Section 623-b)

Your Name (Print, signature not necessary)
Your Address
Your Social Security Number

Cc: Consumer Financial Protection Bureau
Cc: Attorney General's Office
Cc: Better Business Bureau

Letter 2.3 (Creditor Failure to Mark "In Dispute")

Send this letter if the collection agency/creditor provides proof of your signature and claims you are obligated to pay. Wait until the 31st day from which they signed for Letter 1.1 that you mailed. On day 31 check your credit report to see if they show the account as "In Dispute" or "Consumer Disputes this Information". If they did NOT mark it in dispute, proceed with letter 2.3. If they are reporting it in dispute, proceed with letter 2.1.

Date
Your Name
Your Address
Name of creditor/collection agency
Address of creditor/collection agency (from your credit report)
Re: Acct # 123456789

To Whom It May Concern:

The Credit Movement

I recently obtained a copy of my credit report. Much to my dismay, I noticed that you have failed to furnish the credit reporting agencies with the proper and required disclosure with the legally required time period. Under Federal Law, you are required to place the appropriate and necessary remark of "consumer disputes" or "account disputed by consumer" within 30 days of receipt of the dispute request.

According to my records, you signed for the dispute request on [insert date]. My record keeping has been diligent throughout this process in the event the event that you refuse to comply with federal, state, and local laws. I have cc'd the Consumer Financial Protection Bureau ("CFPB"), Office of the Attorney General ("OAG"), and Better Business Bureau ("BBB") as a method of ensuring that you are aware of my intent to file a formal complaint with each if necessary. I will also make my case know via an online public press release of my experience.

Included as evidence I have retained a recent time-stamped credit report along with your signature for the original dispute. These serve to substantiate my claim that you are in clear violation of Fair Credit Reporting Act, Section 623(a)(3) and/or Fair Debt Collection Practices Act Section 807(8) for your refusal to place this required disclosure of "notice of dispute" on my report in the 30 days allowed under the law.

As previously mentioned, I am prepared to take the necessary next steps in the event you fail to clear up this matter as a result of this final goodwill attempt to get you to correct this entirely inaccurate, incomplete, and erroneous item on my credit report. .

For your convenience, I am providing the language from federal law: FCRA 623(a)(3) - Responsibilities of furnishers of information to consumer reporting agencies [15 U.S.C. 1681s-2]

(3) Duty to provide notice of dispute. If the completeness or accuracy of any information furnished by any person to any consumer reporting agency is disputed to such person by a consumer, the person may not furnish the information to any consumer reporting agency without notice that such information is disputed by the consumer.

(B) Time of Notice (I) The notice required under subparagraph (A) shall be provided to the customer prior to, or no later than 30 days after, furnishing the

negative information to a consumer reporting agency described in section 603(p).

As a result of your failure to comply with the aforementioned law by not placing the required disclosures on my credit report, you non-compliance could result in me seeking $1000 in damages per violation in small claims court. Violations, in my best estimate range from Negligent Enablement of Identity Fraud and/or defamation to Violations of both FCRA Section 623 and Violations of FDCPA Section 807.

I would be requesting for you to appear in a court within my local jurisdiction.

Your Name (printed, signature unnecessary)
Your Mailing Address
SSN

Cc: CFPB, OAG, BBB

Letter 2.4 (Bureaus Method of Verification)

You should use this letter if after sending letter 1.2 you get a response from the credit bureaus stated the account was accurate or verified.

Your Name
Your Address
Credit Bureau Name
Credit Bureau Address
Date
RE: Social Security Number: 123456789
To Whom It May Concern:

This purpose of this letter is in response to your recent claim that [insert name of creditor, collection agency, or public record court] has verified that the account they are reporting under my identification is accurate.

Please be advised that I demanding, per my legal right, that the description of the procedure used to determine the completeness, accuracy, and verifiability of the information is requested. This must be provided within fifteen days of the conclusion of your reinvestigation process.

I am requesting that the below detailed and specific information be provided for the individual who supposedly verified this alleged account by providing documentation *bearing my signature.*

Name

Mailing Address

Telephone Number

I am also requesting a copy of any and all documentation provided by the above individual(s) which would constitute a legally binding contract.

I also would like to demand human intervention in this matter and any automated investigation done through systems such as e-oscar is not acceptable in this matter.

I am specifically requesting reinvestigation and your **Method of Verification.**

As always, I am keeping careful records of all communications regarding this matter. Let it also be known that barring any further non-compliance, I am prepared to file formal complaints with the Office of the Attorney General, Consumer Financial Protection Bureau, Better Business Bureau, etc.

For your convenience I remind you of Wenger vs. TransUnion No. 95-6445 (C.D.Cal. Nov. 14, 1995), in which a woman was awarded $200,000 for the willful non-compliance to make necessary changes to the credit report.

As this will be my final attempt to have this inaccuracy corrected, I must make you aware of my intent to go to small claims as necessary.

If court is necessary, I will be seeking the standard $1,000 per violation for:

Negligent Enablement of Identity Fraud
Violating the Fair Credit Reporting Act
Defamation

Your Name (printed or typed, signature unnecessary)
SSN
Address

Cc: CFPB, BBB, Office of Attorney General

Letter 2.5 (Bureaus Failure to Respond in Time)

Send this letter if you do not receive a response from the credit bureaus within 30 days of them signing for letter 1.2.

Your Name
Your Address
Credit Bureau Name
Credit Bureau Address
Date
RE: Social Security Number: 123456789
To Whom It May Concern:

The purpose of this letter is to follow up on a letter I originally sent on [insert date].

The original letter signed for by you on [insert date] was regarding an inaccuracy on my credit report being maintained by your company under on the credit report under my name and social security number.

The account in question is [insert name of creditor/collection agency, or public record reporter].

You have failed to comply with federal law by not responding to my original letter in a timely manner. You have also violated the law by neglecting to provide me with a copy of any evidence **bearing my signature**, which would serve to show the account is being accurately reporting.

Let it be known that I have kept very detailed records of all correspondences regarding this matter and have cc'd the Consumer Financial Protection Bureau ("CFPB"), Office of the Attorney General ("OAG"), and Better Business Bureau ("BBB") — for my protection. Should this final attempt to correct this matter go unresolved, I am prepared to file formal complaints and make a public online press release of my experience.

Let me also remind of a case in which a woman was awarded $200,000 as a result of a credit bureaus failure to correct items on her report. Wenger v. Trans Union Corp., No. 95-6445 (C.D.Cal. Nov. 14, 1995).

Should you refuse to comply with the law and my efforts to amicably correct this obvious error in reporting prove unfruitful, it may result in small claims action against your company. I would likely be seeking a minimum of $1000 for each violation on the grounds of your defamation, negligent enablement of identity fraud, and violations of the Fair Credit Reporting Act.

Your Name (printed or typed, signature unnecessary)
Your Mailing Address
Social Security Number

Cc: CFPB, OAG, BBB

Letter 2.6 (Bureaus Fail to Respond or Verify - Legal Action Intent)

Use this letter if the credit bureaus continue to verify your account or fail to respond. If you do not intend to take legal action against the credit bureaus, skip to letter 2.7.

Your Name
Your Address

Ryan David

Credit Bureau Name
Credit Bureau Address
Date
RE: Social Security Number: 123456789

WARNING — THIS IS MY FINAL COMMUNICATION REGARDING INACCURATE AND ERRONEOUS INFORMATION BE REPORTED BY [INSERT NAME OF CREDITOR/COLLECTION AGENCY/PUBLIC RECORD RECORDER]

I have made numerous exhausting attempts to have you provide evidence ***BEARING MY SIGNATURE,*** to support your reporting — yet again, you have failed to comply and have NOT provided any evidence from [INSERT NAME OF CREDITOR/COLLECTION AGENCY/PUBLIC RECORD RECORDER] to substantiate the accuracy of this account.

I also submitted a letter to you on [INSERT DATE] requesting your "method of verification" — yet again, you have not complied, violating the Fair Credit Reporting Act Section 611(a)(7).

It is my belief that you have failed to act in good faith as a result of your failure to comply with State and Federal Law — for that I have filed a small claims lawsuit against your company. Attached you will find a copy of the lawsuit.

As mentioned in previous requests, I have kept careful records of our correspondences. As a result of my lawsuit, you are required to appear in court. Below is the information regarding the court date and location:

[INSERT COURTHOUSE NAME AND ADDRESS] on [INSERT DATE]

As indicated in previous letters, I am seeking [iNSERT DOLLAR AMOUNT] for damages associated with your Violations of the Fair Credit Reporting Act, particularly section 611.

Should you have a change of heart and decide to correct your reporting and remove the erroneous item, please contact me as soon as possible so I may withdraw my lawsuit as necessary.

Your Name (printed or typed, signature not necessary)
Social Security Number
Mailing Address
Cc: CFPB, OAG, BBB

Letter 2.7 (5 Day Reinsertion Letter)

This letter should be used if the credit bureaus deleted an account and later you noticed that they put it back on your report without notifying you.

Your Name
Your Address
Credit Bureau Name
Credit Bureau Address

Date

RE: Social Security Number: 123456789

To Whom It May Concern,

I originally disputed an account being reported by your company under my social security number on

[INSERT DATE OF ORIGINAL LETTER]. The account disputed was [INSERT NAME OF CREDITOR/COLLECTION AGENCY/PUBLIC RECORD RECORDER].

Based on a correspondence received from your company on [INSERT DATE DELETION NOTIFICATION WAS RECEIVED], the account was deleted.

Much to my dismay, I have now become aware that the account was reinserted onto my consumer credit report.

In accordance with the requirements of the FCRA section 611(a)(5)(B) (ii), you are required to notify me of the reinsertion in writing within 5 business days. For your convenience, here is the language of the law:

(B)Requirements relating to reinsertion of previously deleted material

(ii)Notice to consumer

If any information that has been deleted from a consumer's file pursuant to subparagraph (A) is reinserted in the file, the consumer reporting agency shall notify the consumer of the reinsertion in writing not later than 5 business days after the reinsertion or, if authorized by the consumer for that purpose, by any other means available to the agency.

To date, I have not received this legally required notification. This is a clear and obvious violation of the Fair Credit Reporting Act. Let it be known that I am well aware of my rights — of those is my right to pursue legal action against your company for your disregarding of the law.

This letter is to demand that you delete this account from my credit report. Should you chose not to comply, you are exposed to legal action and I will be filing a formal complaint with the Consumer Financial Protection Bureau ("CFPB"), Office of the Attorney General ("OAG"), and Better Business Bureau ("BBB").

Your Name (printed or typed, signature not required)
Your SSN
Your Mailing Address
Cc: CFPB, OAG, BBB

Chapter 4:
Enhanced Techniques

Public Records

For obvious reasons, public records items will kill your credit score. Public records include bankruptcies, tax liens, and judgements.

Removing Public Record Information from Your Report

Public Record data is reported to Experian, Equifax, and Transunion by a data collection firm called LexisNexis. This is important to note because this simple fact presents you with an opportunity to have certain public record information removed from your credit reports with Experian, Equifax and Transunion. Remember, under the Fair Credit Reporting Act the information maintained within your credit report must be complete, accurate and verifiable. Also, remember that often times when you dispute an item on your credit report that the dispute gets processed electronically using a software called e-oscar.

One of the pieces of information within your credit report that must be accurately documented is who furnished the information to the credit bureau. When it comes to public record data it often lists the furnisher as *Recorder of Deeds, Clerk of Courts, Municipal Court, or Magistrate.* This is where there is an opportunity for you to have the information removed.

Countless times the readers of this book and presumably many others are told by the courts that they do not provide or furnish information to the credit bureaus — so why do the credit bureaus list the courts as the provider? Great question! While the court may be the one where the public information was sourced by LexisNexis, it is not the entity furnishing that information directly to the bureaus. Essentially how it works is, LexisNexis "mines" all the public record details from all accessible public portals and then sells that information to Experian, Equifax, and Transunion. There is huge profit in mining and furnishing data!

Regardless, this presents you with the opportunity to get the public record removed at a credit bureau level. Here what you need to do:

1. Write a letter to the appropriate Clerk of Courts
2. In letter request the procedure used to verify record with Experian, Equifax, and Transunion

3. Include an envelope with your address and a stamp on it to encourage a fast response
4. Once you receive their letter stating they do not report to the credit bureaus you have what you need to send to the bureaus requesting removal of the inaccurate data for their violation of the FCRA.

Tax Liens

Tax Liens occur as a result of the governments legal claim against your property until an unpaid tax debt is satisfied. The government can legally take away your property to satisfy an unpaid tax debt. Tax liens can come as a surprise to many as they may not even be aware of the tax debt. For instance, often times when a debt is forgiven the creditor will file a 1099-C form which you will be required to then claim that forgiven amount as income on your taxes. For instance, if you owe $1000 on a credit card debt and settle the debt for $200, you may receive a 1099-C requiring you to pay taxes on the $800 that was forgiven. Neglecting to pay these types of taxes is often the cause for tax liens. Failure to pay ordinary income tax is another common way that tax liens end up haunting your credit report and score. Failure by your employer to properly pay payroll taxes may also result in tax liens.

One bit of positive news is that as of July 1, 2017 Experian, Equifax, and Transunion announced that they will be removing tax liens and judgements that do not meet basic reporting criteria — name, mailing address, social security number, and birthdate. Many tax liens and judgements have already been eliminated from consumer credit reports!

Another bit of good news is the the IRS has something called the "Fresh Start" initiative in which you can qualify to have a lien removed from your credit report once you have establishment a repayment schedule for your tax debt or once the debt has been satisfied. In order to qualify to have it removed from your credit report once the debt has been satisfied, you must meet certain criteria: You must have properly followed the law and filed all appropriate business, individual, and information returns over the past 3 years, and you are current on all estimated payments and IRS federal tax payments.

In order to qualify for the *Fresh Start* initiative while still making payments you must meet even more criteria, but it is possible; total debt must be under $25,000, you have set up the direct-debit installment program agreeing to pay off debt within 60 months or less, you have made at least 3 consecutive payments and made all payments as agreed, and have never defaulted on your direct debit program.

If you feel you meet either of these criteria you can proceed with attempting to have your tax liens expunged from your report by:

1. If you do not have it, request a copy of IRS Form 668(Z), Release of Federal Tax Lien. You should have received this after satisfying your lien or being granted waiver of any unpaid balance.
2. Gather your original paperwork regarding the Notice of Federal Tax Lien. Form 668(Y).
3. Fill out Form 12277. Application for Withdrawal of Filed Form 668(Y).
4. Now that you have gathered and/or filled out IRS Forms 668(Z), 668(Y), and 12277 — you must submit all three to the IRS. Include a detailed explanation stating that you are requesting the lien be withdrawn and why.
5. Remember the IRS does not move quickly but you should eventually receive IRS Form 10916(c). Withdrawal of Filed Notice of Federal Tax Lien.
6. Call the IRS to check on the status of your request if nothing is received after 3 weeks.
7. Once you have Form 10916(c), promptly send it to Experian, Equifax, and Transunion.

Repossessions

A vehicle repossession can be very detrimental to your credit. Whether voluntary or involuntary, a repo can murder your credit score. Remember, just because an action on your credit took place and is accurate — that does not mean that the consumer protection laws have been followed and/or the reporting of the account is legitimate.

Be sure to gather all documentation regarding the repossessed vehicle, including: the original retail installment sales agreement for lease or purchase of vehicle, all loan payment details and records, all repair or service receipts, and all documents and correspondences from dealer or lender. These documents may be needed if you need to take legal action or defend yourself against legal action.

Lenders are not allowed to *breach the peace* when repo'ing a vehicle. The courts will often review the circumstances of the actual capturing of the vehicle to determine breaching of the peace. For instance — whether the owner was physically present, whether the repossessing company entered the property of the owner without consent, and/or was use of force or violent threats used to repo the vehicle. The lender and repo company could be liable for damages in the event a breach of peach took place.

Lenders are not allowed to violate Military Service Protection. A lender is not allowed to repossess the vehicle of an active duty service member without court approval. If they do, they could be subject to civil and criminal charges.

Improper calculation of deficiency balances is a common theme in the world of car repossessions. It is important that you gather all documents, contracts and loan payment history to ensure the lender properly calculated any claims against you, such as:

* Interest Rate: Does it match what the lender is legally allowed to charge under the laws of your state?
* Late Fees and Charges: Do any lender fees match the original agreement? Are they accurate late charges?
* Payments and Credits: Did the lender properly credit you for all payments made as agreed?
* Attorney Fees: Does your agreement allow the lender to pass attorney fees onto you? Does your state allow

them to pass these fees as part of the deficiency balance?

* Repo and Storage Fees: Are repo and storage fees disclosed in your original agreement? Each state places limits on these fees. Research if these fees are allowed in your state and what the limits are.

It is possible that a creditor is completely barred from collecting a deficiency balance. This is typically the case if the lender failed to provide required written notices, failed to conduct the sale of the car in a commercially reasonable manner, or refused to allow you an opportunity to reinstate the loan. If you happened to include the car debt in a bankruptcy they may also be barred from collecting on the deficiency balance.

Lenders must legally provide certain notices following the repossession of a vehicle. The first notice is with respect to *redemption* and the second is regarding the *deficiency balance.*

Following the repo of a vehicle, a *Notice of Sale* is issued if you do not make an attempt to get your vehicle back prior to the vehicle being sold at auction or otherwise. Most states afford consumers a *right to cure,* which gives the opportunity to bring the account current and get their vehicle back. In most states, lenders must provide the notice of sale at least 10 days prior to sale of the car — giving you a reasonable amount of time to bring the loan current or pay off the loan and repo fees to get the vehicle back. If the lender does not provide this required notice a court may deem the deficiency balance non-collectable.

The second required notice following the sale of the vehicle is a statement regarding the deficiency balance. This notice must include the amount the lender credited you with the proceeds of the sale, and a notification of cancelation of the original sales agreement. Many repossessed vehicles are sold well below market resale value at wholesale auctions. If your vehicle was sold below market value at an auction, you can dispute this in court to be rewarded the difference between the resale price and fair and reasonable market value.

Lenders and car dealers are required to conform with the Uniform Commercial Code, Consumer Fraud Act, Truth in Lending Act, and Retail Installment Sales Act. The below letters will reference these statutes.

Letter 3.1 - Send to Original Creditor, Collection Agency, and Car Dealership

Ryan David

Your Name
Your Address
Collection Agency Name & Address
Original Creditor Name & Address
Car Dealer Name & Address
Date
RE: VIN # [insert vin # here]

To Whom It May Concern:

This letter serves as a formal statement to notify the above referenced companies of the dispute of the accounts pertaining to the vehicle under VIN # [insert vin # here].

The vehicle attached to the above referenced VIN was purchased on or around [INSERT DATE]. The financing was done by [INSERT FINANCE COMPANY NAME]. The vehicle in question was repossessed in the state of [INSERT STATE] and sold by [INSERT CREDITOR/COMPANY NAME] on or around [INSERT DATE].

As I am sure you are aware, according to UCC § 9.506 as well as State RISA and MVISA statutes, a deficiency can not be claimed unless all of the required notices were properly and timely given, and all of the allowable redemption and cure time limits were adhered to.

I am demanding proof that the above referenced vehicle was repossessed legally and in accordance with following UCC:

- *§ 9-506. EFFECT OF ERRORS OR OMISSIONS.*

- *§ 9-611. NOTIFICATION BEFORE DISPOSITION OF COLLATERAL*

- *§ 9-612. TIMELINESS OF NOTIFICATION BEFORE DISPOSITION OF COLLATERAL.*

- *§ 9-613. CONTENTS AND FORM OF NOTIFICATION BEFORE DISPOSITION OF COLLATERAL*

I am demanding that you comply with your legal requirement to provide me with copies of any legal notices and any and all notifications regarding the resale of the subject vehicle.

If you are unable to produce the proof within fifteen (15) days of the receipt of this certified document, the alleged claim of a deficiency balance owed will be immediately considered null and void. If any collection efforts continue, or if this invalid alleged account remains on my credit report, you will be in violation of the Fair Debt Collection Practices Act and the Fair Credit Reporting Act.

Under State and Federal statutes, I reserve the right to seek damages against all parties including, not limited to UCC § 9-625 remedies, if you fail to comply with the above demands.

Additionally, I am requesting that you and/or your representatives immediately cease and desist any further reporting or communication regarding this matter with the exception of the US Postal Service.

å

Cc: CFPB, Office of the Attorney General, BB

Letter 3.2 - Send to Credit Bureau 14 days after sending letter 3.1

Your Name

Your Address
Credit Bureau Name
Credit Bureau Address
Date
RE: SSN # [insert SSN # here]

I am writing this letter as a result of becoming aware of an account that is being illegally reported on my credit report report under the social security number listed above. The account in question is being reported by [insert company name] under account # [insert account number]. I issued a formal dispute of this account directly with [insert company name] referencing their illegal and unlawful reporting regards to their illegal reporting. To date, I have not received a reply to my formal inquiry.

As a result of their failure to comply with the law, nor respond in a timely manner, I am issuing this investigation request to you directly. Under the Fair Credit Reporting Act, I have every right to request your *Method of Verification.* This would include the name and contact information of any individual you spoke with to reach any conclusion in reference to the account in question.

Please note, I have always kept organized records and documentation of all correspondences regarding this matter. In the event, this issue is not resolved to my satisfaction, or per the law, I will be forced to file a formal complaint with the Office of the Attorney General ("OAG"), the Consumer Financial Protection Bureau ("CFPB"), and the Better Business Bureau ("BBB").

Your Name (printed, signature not required)

Your Social Security #

Your Mailing Address

Cc: CFPB, Office of the Attorney General, BBB

Medical Debts and HIPPA Privacy Laws

If after sending your group 1 letters, you receive a copy of the medical bill and/or are being harassed by a collection agency — it is likely that they cannot provide proof that they have an agreement to collect on behalf of the health care provider, or a signed contract binding you to the debt. The other leverage you may have is if the medical bill shows your personal medical data, and this is a serious violation of the Health Insurance

Portability and Accountability Act of 1996 (HIPAA). Privacy laws are on your side and prohibit the disclosing of personal health information without your consent. Any release of information regarding your condition would break this privacy law. If they indeed did release your health information you are in the drivers seat as this creates a problem for the collection agency and health care provider. The following letters are designed to help you remove those erroneous medical collections.

__Letter 3.3__ - HIPAA letter to send to Health Care Provider

Your Name
Your Address
Credit Bureau Name
Credit Bureau Address
Date
RE: SSN # [insert SSN # here]

I am writing this letter as a result of becoming aware of an account that is being illegally reported on my credit report report under the social security number listed above. The account in question is being reported by [insert company name] under account # [insert account number]. I issued a formal dispute of this account directly with [insert company name] referencing their illegal and unlawful reporting regards to their illegal reporting. To date, I have not received a reply to my formal inquiry.

As a result of their failure to comply with the law, nor respond in a timely manner, I am issuing this investigation request to you directly. Under the Fair Credit Reporting Act, I have every right to request your **Method of Verification.** This would include the name and contact information of any individual you spoke with to reach any conclusion in reference to the account in question.

Please note, I have always kept organized records and documentation of all correspondences regarding this matter. In the event, this issue is not resolved to my satisfaction, or per the law, I will be forced to file a formal complaint with the Office of the Attorney General ("OAG"), the Consumer Financial Protection Bureau ("CFPB"), and the Better Business Bureau ("BBB").

Your Name (printed, signature not required)

Your Social Security #

Your Mailing Address

Cc: CFPB, Office of the Attorney General, BBB

Letter 3.4 - HIPPA letter for collection validation, dispute, cease and desist

Your Name
Your Address
Collection Agency Name
Collection Agency Address
Date
Re: Acct # 123456789
To Whom It May Concern:

This notice is being sent as a formal **dispute** in response to a letter that you recently sent. This does not serve as a notice of *refusal* to *pay*, but rather to notify you of a dispute of the claims within your letter, and a formal request for validation of the alleged debt.

The Fair Debt Collection Practices Act ("FDCPA") allows me the right to request the aforementioned validation of the alleged debt.

All this notice to serve as my formal request for proof that the alleged debt belongs to me. I am requesting the following information regarding this debt:

- Date of the alleged medical service
- Name of the patient receiving service
- Proof of a binding contractual obligation to pay alleged debt

As evidence to support any satisfaction of the above information request, please provide viable documentation, such as:

- Agreement between the medical service provider and your company, which would grant you the authority to collect on behalf of your client for the alleged debt.
- Proof of your acquisition of the debt or...
- Proof of your contractual assignment to collect alleged debt
- Authorization under subtitle D of the ARRA, Section 13401.
- Proof, *bearing the signature* the alleged debtor wherein they agreed to pay the alleged creditor.

- Being this is a medical debt, a copy of the HIPAA authorization

Application of Security Provisions and Penalties to Business Associates of Covered Entities; and Sections 13407(1) Breach of Security.

Wish respect to the term "Breach of Security", unsecured identifiable health information of an individual in a personal health record, acquisition of such information without the prior authorization of that individual, constitutes a Breach of Security.

It is worth noting that the aforementioned liabilities fall directly under the penalty guidelines and rules of the Omnibus Final Rule, made effective 09/23/2013. The implementation of such provisions of the Health Information Technology for Economic and Clinical Health Act of 2009 (HITECH Act) which was issued 11/30/2009.

This letter should not only serve as my notice of dispute with regards to the letter sent, but also as a notice to cease and desist all collection activities and reporting of the alleged debt to the credit reporting agencies.

I am demanding your compliance with the specific request of this letter within thirty (30) days — failure must result in a total and complete removal of all claims and I must be notified in writing within the timeframe requested.

Your failure to respond or any non-compliance may result in a small claims suit, complaints being filed with the OCR regarding HIPAA violations, Consumer Financial Protection Bureau, RipoffReport.com, the BBB, as well as applicable bar associations, the Office of the Attorney General, and the FTC for violations of the Fair Credit Reporting Act and Fair Debt Collections Practices Act.

Let it also be known that I reserve my right to take private civil action against you to recover damages for any and all violations.

Regards,
Name (printed, signature not required)

Student Loans

It is no secret that Americans as a whole are struggling to repay their student loans. Higher education costs are soaring. Our world is changing, corporations have access to cheaper labor overseas, technology and automation are advancing — this leads to lower salaries and less demand for human resources. In my opinion, higher education is bordering on 'not being worth it'.

Student loan debt is overwhelming for many of you. Your income can barely support your day-to-day needs and there is no money left to pay back those looming student loans. You may even feel taken advantage of by the "system". You have been told that college is the answer. I'm of the belief that this is a thought of previous generations and that train of thought will soon shift in the mainstream.

Many of you wish you could make your student loans disappear with the snap of a finger — we know that is not possible — so now what?

If you look in the right places, you will find a variety of options for repayment plans, or even forgiveness of your student loans. There are various student loan forgiveness programs out there for people who work in certain fields, such as; education, public service, and other types of employment. Some state and local governments even help their debt-ridden graduates pay off their loans.

Forgiveness and Income Based Repayment Programs are available if you know where to look and how to apply. These aren't just for those crushed under six-figure student loan debt, but also those looking for "free money" to help relieve the burden of your student loans. A great resource chalked full of information is available at http://StudentLoanHero.com.

Evictions

Rental property evictions and collections arising from "damages" to the property or early termination of the lease can be very detrimental to your score. They can hinder your ability to get a rental property or home loan in the future — potentially putting yourself and/or your family in a very difficult situation. Challenging these types of accounts for removal can be difficult, but not impossible. Property Management companies are notorious for keeping poor records and making errors in the way they report collection accounts. Also, they often violate the Fair Debt Collection Practices Act in their efforts to collect on the debt. With a keen eye you can identify inaccuracies and challenge them for removal. If you do not have it, request a copy of the original lease you signed. Then, get your hands on a copy of an itemized list of what you supposedly owe from the property manager.

Be sure that any fees, penalties, damages, and other charges are accurate and jive with the original contract/lease you signed. If the debt has been sold or transferred to a third party collection agency or law firm be sure they provided legal proof (dunning letter/debt validation letter) that they have the right to collect on the debt. They must also provide the detailed summery of how they calculated the amount they are claiming that you owe. After identifying any discrepancies, inconsistencies, or errors — dispute the debt with the 3 credit bureaus. Here is the dispute letter you should use to challenge the eviction account.

Ryan David

Name of Property Manager
Address of Prop Mgr
City, State Zip

Account #

Dear {Prop Mgr},

The above referenced account in my name is reporting to Experian, Equifax, and Transunion. I find this hard to believe as I do not owe your company any money. Additionally, I have never been contacted by your company with respect to this alleged debt. That being the case, I don't quite understand why you continue to violate my consumer rights by damaging my credit rating without properly validating the alleged debt.

According to your reporting to the credit bureaus I owe you money — How much? What is this alleged debt for? When did you supply supporting documentation verifying that I owe the alleged amount? Specifically, how did you come up with the amount you are claiming that I owe? Where is the legal proof that you have the right to collect from me in the first place?

As previously stated, I am completely unaware of this alleged debt. See this letter as notification that I reject your request to do business. I am challenging your legal authority to collect this alleged debt. Additionally, I am requesting that you cease and desist, return this account to the appropriate party and remove this account from my credit report.

Thirty days should be a sufficient amount of time to supply legal supporting documents or remove this from my credit report.

Regards,

Your Name
Your Social Security Number

116

Settling Collections

Always remember that simply paying a collection does not improve your credit score. Often times, paying a collection can actually lower your credit score. Why? The algorithm used to calculate your credit score is an imperfect system. A collection is given a coding such as "O-9" or "I-9". This two digit coding tells the algorithm "we have something bad", and in order to determine how bad it is (how much it negatively impacts your credit score) the algorithm looks at the "date of last activity" on the account. The more recent the date of last activity, the more the account will negatively impact your score. That date can only be reset by you making a payment.

Our membership website offers an easy-to-follow guide on what to do if you have collections that you would like to pay. In the "Handling Collections" online course I will walk you through exactly what to do to ensure you properly handle your collections.

Filing Complaints (BBB, CFPB, Office of Attorney General)

Filing formal complaints is an effective way to get the credit bureaus or your creditors to take action on your requests. It is important to follow through on filing complaints if you are not getting your desired results using the letters in the book.

Filing formal complaints is easily done online. Be as detailed as possible!

To file a complaint with the Better Business Bureau go to:

Go to **https://www.bbb.org/consumer-complaints/file-a-complaint/get-started**

Better Business Bureau® Start With Trust® | Online Complaint System

BBB.org   Contact Us

What complaints do we handle?

Disputes that relate to marketplace issues experienced with the services or products a business provides. BBB reserves the right to reject complaints that use abusive or foul language.

We do not handle:

- Employee/employer disputes;
- Discrimination claims;
- Matters that are/have been litigated/arbitrated;
- Complaints against individuals not engaged in business;
- Issues challenging the validity of local, state, or federal law;
- Complaints against government agencies, including the postal service;
- Matters not related to marketplace issues.

How do we handle your complaint?

Everything you submit will be forwarded to the business within two business days. The business will be asked to respond within 14 days, and if a response is not received, a second request will be made. You will be notified of the business's response when we receive it (or notified that we received no response). Complaints are usually closed within 30 business days.

BBBs accept complaints that meet the following criteria:

- The complaint includes the complainant's name, a postal address, and an email address
- The complaint includes the business's name and provides sufficient information to determine the business's location
- The complaint seeks assistance from BBB
- The complaint is from a person (or a person's authorized representative) or entity (business-to-business) that had a marketplace "relationship"
- The complaint relates to a marketplace issue. Typically, the issue complained of must have arisen within the previous 12 months (Note: warranties/guarantees or other extenuating circumstances may supersede this criteria.)
- The complaint must allege a deficiency in the company's marketplace performance with regard to the services or products at the business provided or allegedly agreed to provide
- The complaint is not in litigation when filed with BBB and has not been resolved by a previous court action, arbitration, or settlement between the parties
- The complaint contains no abusive language.

To file a complaint with the Consumer Financial Protection Bureau go to:

https://www.consumerfinance.gov/complaint/getting-started/

Submit a complaint

There are five steps to submit your complaint:

Step 1: What is this complaint about?

Step 2: What type of problem are you having?

Step 3: What happened?

Step 4: What company is this complaint about?

Step 5: Who are the people involved?

Before you get started

You'll need the dates, amounts, and other details about your complaint. If you have documents you want to include, such as billing statements or letters from the company, you'll be able to attach them in Step 3.

Make sure to include all the information you can, because you generally can't submit a second complaint about the same problem.

We'll forward your complaint and any documents you provide to the company and work to get you a response – generally within 15 days.

Start your complaint

To file a complaint with the Office of The Attorney General:

Find out where the company you are filing the complaint about is headquartered. Google where to file an Attorney General complaint for that state. Most states allow you to file the complaint online.

Lawsuits and Small Claims

It is always advisable to seek the advice and counsel of an attorney when considering a lawsuit. It is rare that your situation will need to resort to legal action and our hope is that the letters and advice within this book will help resolve your credit concerns without it coming to a legal battle. That being said, many readers have elected to, and had success with visiting their local courthouse and file a small claims lawsuits.

Filing a Small Claims lawsuit is a fairly simple process and only requires a few minutes of your time and a small filing fee. Fair Credit Reporting Act rules allow for you to seek up to $1000 per violation. The filing fee often depends on the amount you are seeking. Remember, the ultimate goal is to remove derogatory and erroneous items from your credit report.

Our membership site offers more information and a step-by-step course on lawsuits. You will also find video tutorials in our private Facebook community.

Chapter 5:
Building Positive, Open, Active Credit

Building positive, open, active credit is just as important as addressing the negative items on your credit report. That being said, getting approved for credit can be a challenge when you are already in a tough spot. That is why you must get creative. This chapter will share resources of creditors that offer financing to those with less than stellar credit scores. I will also share little known tricks that can help you get positive credit lines showing up on your report.

Secured Credit Cards

Secured Credit Cards is a common starting point for many seeking to either build or re-build their credit report. "Secured" means that the card is collateralized by your cash. As a general rule, the worse your credit score, the higher the required deposit. Prove your credit worthiness with secured cards and other opportunities for unsecured credit is right around the corner. I have researched all the available secured cards, their annual fees, deposit requirements, etc. — Here is a list for you to analyze and make your decision on which are best for you.

Horizon Gold Card

https://www.horizoncardservices.com/a/pg3_app.php

* No Employment Check
* Guaranteed $500 unsecured credit limit
* No Credit Check
* Online Application
* Reports to Major Credit Bureau

Milestone Gold Card
https://www.milestonegoldcard.com/get-your-gold-card

* Annual Fee between $35 and $75 depending on credit score
* Mastercard Gold Benefits
* 24/7 Account Access and Bill Pay
*

OpenSky Secured Visa
https://www.openskycc.com/Applet.aspx

* Reports Monthly to All 3 Bureaus

* Credit Line from $200-$3000 based on deposit
* No Credit History Required
* No Credit Check
* No Processing or Application Fees
* Visa Logo

OpenSky®

✓ Rebuild Credit

✓ Take control

✓ Meet your financial goals

Reports monthly to all 3 major credit bureaus—
builds your credit quickly through responsible use.

- Credit line as low as $200 up to $3000, linked to your fully refundable security deposit
- No credit history required to apply
- No credit check and no checking account necessary
- No fees for application and processing
- Accepted everywhere you see the Visa logo

NAME

| First | Initial(opt.) | Last |

| Email | A valid email address is required to complete this application as it is the primary method by which we will contact you. |

SelfLender.com

SelfLender is a relatively new phenomena — but an effective credit building tool.

SelfLender is an "installment loan" form of credit. The shopping cart loophole, secured credit cards, and the authorized user trick are all "revolving" forms of credit.

The SelfLender.com credit builder account works the opposite of most installment accounts. With most loans, you receive the money and then make payments. With SelfLender, you make your payments and get the money afterwards. All loan payments are reported to the three major credit reporting agencies.

Visit **https://www.selflender.com/signup**

Authorized User Trick

Having a spouse, friend, neighbor, or relative add you as an authorized user on their already existing credit card is a great way to build your positive credit. When being added as an authorized user, the bank or credit card company does not pull your credit so you do not need to fear being denied. The reason they do not pull your credit is because as an authorized user you are not responsible for the payment. My father added my little brother to his credit card to boost his score so he could purchase a home. The card my dad added my brother to had been open since 1983 — my brother was 29 years old and had 33 years of credit history!

Remember "Length of Credit History" is 15% of your overall credit score. While this certainly helped my brother in this case, there are a few things to aware of, and rules to follow when being added as an authorized user:

1. Make sure the card has a balance that is less than 30% of the limit

2. The longer the card has been open, the better. 2 years + minimum

3. Be sure the card has perfect payment history (no late payments)

4. Be aware that if they max out the card or go late, you will suffer

5. Immediately remove yourself if #4 happens

6. Don't rely only on authorized user accounts, build more credit

7. If you don't do #6, home loan lenders may deny you or request removal of the authorized user account

Making Use of Small Banks and Credit Unions

Smaller local and regional banks as well as credit unions are great resources for those with less than stellar credit.

They often offer products to credit-challenged folks without the scrutiny of more mainstream banks. Interest rates and account fees are often more favorable with smaller institutions.

Pentagon Federal Credit Union, Navy Federal Credit Union, and USAA are more likely to offer higher limit secured and unsecured credit cards. Often times, becoming a member of one of these military-affiliated Banks or Credit Unions can be a challenge if you or an immediate family member did not serve in a branch of the military. Don't worry, you can still get in and become a member so you can take advantage of ALL they have to offer. Below are steps to become a member of a non-profit organization that will allow you to gain access to military-affiliated institutions.

Step 1

Become a member of the Navy League of San Diego. Visit the website below. Fill out the application.

https://join.navyleague.org/wordpress/membership-form/

The Credit Movement

The Navy League is a non-profit organization supporting America's sea services such as; Coast Guard, Marine Corps, and the Navy. They have several branches, referred to as a "Council".

It is important that you select the San Diego Council —this is the only chapter that non-military members are accepted into certain banks or credit unions

When you get to the part of the form shown below, be sure to select San Diego as your council.

Citizenship

U.S. Citizen   NOT a U.S. Citizen

You will be assigned a Council based on your zip code unless you have a preferred council.

Preferred Council, if you have one

Council Locator

Do you have a sponsor?

Sponsor's Name

Type sponsor's name here.

Credit Card Payment

This is a secure server. We do not store your credit card information. You may also join by calling (800) 356-5760, faxing your completed membership form to (703) 528-2333, or printing and mailing the completed PDF form from the link above to the address on the printed form.

Please ensure your address zip code entered above matches the credit card billing address zip code for your payment to be correctly processed.

Membership Team
Navy League of the United States
2300 Wilson Blvd, Suite 200
Arlington, VA 22201

Step 2

After completing the application and paying your $25 membership fee (tax-deductible by the way), be sure to print out your confirmation receipt and the email you will receive.

Step 3

Now you have the necessary military affiliation proof you need to apply for membership with USAA, Navy Federal Credit Union, and PenFed.

A good place to start is by applying to Pentagon Federal Credit Union. Members of The Credit Movement are being approved for auto loans and huge credit card limits from PenFed as you are reading this. Start building your credit with PenFed today! Go here:

https://netmember.penfed.org/NetMember/Forms/OpenAccounts/Eligibility.aspx?MEMBERSHIP

Step 4

Fill out the online application.

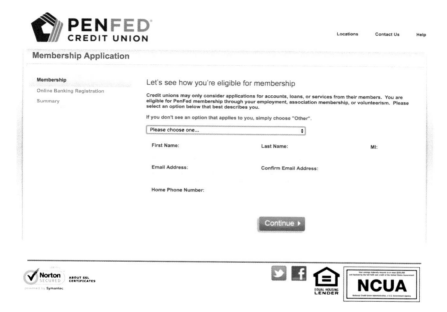

The first drop down ask you to select how you are eligible for membership. Select "I belong to the following association or organization"

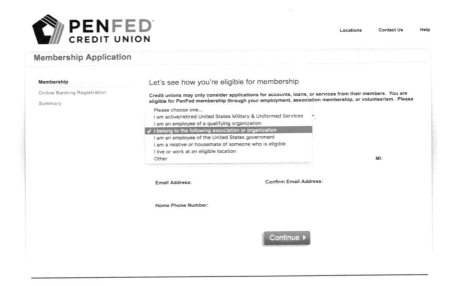

Then select "Navy League of the United States".

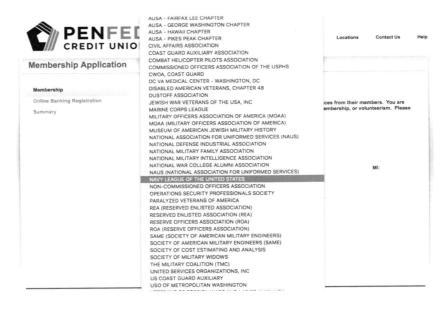

Step 5

You will need a debit/credit card to fund your membership account with $5 bucks. You must maintain a minimum balance of $5 for the duration of your membership. Remember that once you've joined PenFed and any other military-affiliated institutions, you can cancel your qualifying membership. Once you're a member of these banks, you're a member for life.

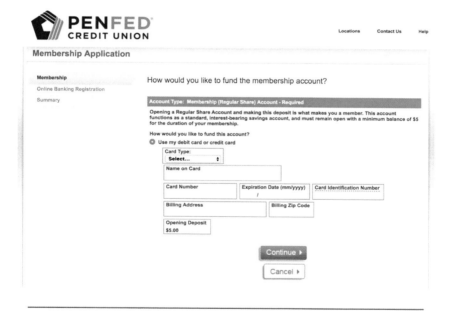

Step 6

CALL them and apply for some credit! DO NOT APPLY ONLINE! Why?

If you have negative items on your credit report, the automated systems that they use to determine eligibility may automatically disqualify you. When you call, they often allow you to explain the items and can make a manual approval or make an exception.

Shopping Cart Loophole

The shopping cart loophole is another creative way to get positive, open, active credit reporting. Be sure to clear browser history and disable pop up blockers before trying this. Also, if they ever ask for your full social security number, abort mission and try another website. This only works when they ask for the last 4 digits of your social.

You have likely at some point received something in your mailbox from a credit card company or insurance company that said, "You have been pre-approved!" Credit card and insurance companies access your credit via a "soft" credit check known as a "promotional inquiry". The shopping cart loophole works similarly.

When placing items in the shopping cart, the merchant is utilizing a "soft" credit inquiry technology to pre-approve you for their credit card offer.

Here are a few places you could try that have worked for others in The Credit Movement Community:

Buckle Credit Card
http://www.buckle.com
Eddie Bauer Credit Card
http://www.eddiebauer.com
Express Credit Card
http://www.express.com
GameStop
http://www.gamestop.com
Home Shopping Network (HSN)
http://www.hsn.com
J.Crew
http://www.jcrew.com
LOFT Credit Card
http://www.loft.com
New York & Co. Rewards Credit Card

http://nyandcompany.com

Pier 1 Credit Card
http://www.pier1.com

Pottery Barn Kids Credit Card
http://www.potterybarnkids.com

Pottery Barn Credit Card
http://www.potterybarn.com

Restoration Hardware Credit Card
https://restorationhardware.com

Victoria's Secret Credit Card
https://www.victoriassecret.com

This is just a sampling. You can try this on any site you would like.

Here is a step-by-step guide to this little known loophole.

Step 1

Clear your browser history, cookies and cache. This is a must-do step as it is imperative that your information does not repopulate into the shopping cart. Open your internet browser and look for "History" in the top toolbar. Then clear all history, cookies, and cache.

Step 2

Disable Pop-Up Blockers. This can usually be found in the "Tools" drop down in your browser toolbar up top. This is an important step as many of the shopping cart loophole offers use pop-up technology.

Step 3

Set up a new account on the website of the credit card you would like to get. Most places will allow you to set up an account free of charge. You could also opt-in to their rewards or loyalty type of program. Be sure when you enter your information that it appears exactly as you believe it appears on your credit report. If they offer a newsletter or email opt-in, I suggest doing that in the event they send offers of pre-qualification or pre-approval to their email subscribers. As you will notice, Synchrony Bank is the "money" behind many of the cards listed below. Getting approved for one may make it easier to get approved for others that are using the same backend bank.

Step 4

Shop around on the page and place some items in the shopping cart. It seems like $100 is the magic number. If you are not prompted when placing $100 worth of merchandise in the shopping cart, try to add or subtract items in $50 increments. You may not be prompted until you begin the checkout the process.

Step 5

Start the checkout as if you were going to make the purchase. Put your information in but be sure to be deliberate and type slowly. The reason we cleared history in step 1 was so the information does not autofill — if you are prompted to autofill, decline. If it asks for your FULL social security number, log out and try another website. This only works when they only ask for the last 4 digits of your social. When prompted, complete the application. When complete the site will take you back to the checkout page — you can close the page at that point and not make the purchase. Your work is done and the card will likely come in the mail within a week or so.

Remember, you do NOT have to actually proceed with purchases for this to work. Members of the community love this trick because they do not have to apply for credit and get punished for the inquiry 3-5 points only to be declined!

Store Credit Cards

Although store cards are not ideal because they are not versatile forms of credit and can only be used at a particular store, many of these cards are backed by places like Citibank and Capital One, or HSBC — meaning it is likely they will be reported to all three credit bureaus. Remember, it is important that we do whatever possible to get between 3-8 positive accounts to report in order to start working towards the 700 Club!

Overdraft Protection Trick

Most banks and credit cards offer overdraft protection. Sometimes it is referred to as a "cash reserve". Why this is included in the book is because many of these institutions will report the overdraft protection to the credit bureaus as a "Line of Credit". This serves as yet another opportunity to get good credit to show up when the deck is stacked against you. Contact your current bank or other local banks and credit unions to see if they offer overdraft protection and ask if they report to the credit bureaus. Remember, it only helps if they report it to the bureaus. It goes without saying that you do not want to use the overdraft protection if possible.

Conclusion

From the bottom of my heart, I thank you for taking the time to read The Credit Movement Book! It has been my absolute pleasure to share with you the tips, tricks, and techniques I have learned over many years of helping thousands of individuals just like you. I sincerely hope that you will continue to take advantage of the lessons within the book, the courses available on the membership site, and the private Facebook community. I wish you a happy and healthy financial future.